HAPPINESS IS
NOT AN ACCIDENT

HAPPINESS IS NOT AN ACCIDENT

RICHARD W. DE HAAN

ZONDERVAN PUBLISHING HOUSE
GRAND RAPIDS, MICHIGAN

CONTENTS

Part I

HAPPINESS IS NOT AN ACCIDENT

Part II

HAPPINESS IN A CHANGING WORLD

Part III

HAPPINESS IN SPITE OF ADVERSITY

Part IV

HAPPINESS WITH YOURSELF AND OTHERS

Part I

HAPPINESS IS
NOT AN ACCIDENT

1

THE BASIS OF A HAPPY LIFE

Everyone desires happiness, but relatively few people find it. Social workers, pastors, psychiatrists, and psychologists fill their hours trying to help desperate, unhappy people. Americans spend billions on new homes, furniture, appliances, autos, and recreational equipment. A variety of radio and television programs are available to multitudes at the switch of a dial, and people while away their spare hours with sporting events, professional jokesters, and other forms of entertainment. Yet no age has ever seen so much unhappiness! Nervous breakdowns, suicides, broken homes, drug addiction, alcoholism, and unrest are the hallmarks of our time. Behind the facade of gaiety and the appearance of well-being lies a deep and pervading sense of loneliness and anxiety. Why are people so unhappy? The answer may be found in the Bible. It tells us that although man was created in the likeness of God, and was designed to live a holy life in fellowship with his Maker, he is now a fallen, sinful creature, alienated from God and needing forgiveness. Augustine was right when he wrote in his famous *Confessions*, "Thou madest us for thyself, and we shall never find rest save as we rest in Thee."

The first step toward a happy life must be a spiritual one. If you desire escape from frustration, failure, and fear, you must be right with God. You need to have confidence in His existence, possess the assurance of sins forgiven, and receive strength to overcome the evils that mar your life.

I. FAITH

The Bible emphasizes the importance of believing, telling us that without faith it is impossible to please God (Hebrews 11:6). This faith is more than a vague belief that some kind of higher power exists, and that in some way all things eventually will work out well. Biblical faith is not mere wishful thinking. Grounded in history, it has intellectual content and involves the entire personality of the one who possesses it.

The faith of which the Bible speaks is not a blind, irrational leap, but a reasonable step based upon sound evidence. Actually, the naturalist is the one who has taken an illogical position requiring blind faith. He is at a complete loss to explain how intelligent life came about through sheer accident, and is baffled by the second law of thermodynamics, which demands a *time* for creation. For example, scientists agree that the sun is gradually losing its heat, and one is forced to conclude that our sun was put in its place recently enough to still be effective today. Never forget that some of the greatest scientists are men of faith, convinced that the Designer and Creator of the universe is the God revealed in the Bible.

The faith in God that brings happiness, however, does not rest upon these evidences. Rather, it is grounded upon God's revelation of Himself through the Son, as recorded in the Bible. Almost 2000 years ago Jesus Christ appeared on this earth, claimed to be the fulfillment of Old Testament prophecies, and declared Himself to be God. He said He would die for the salvation of sinners, asserted He would rise the third day, and gave credence to His claims by His miracles and teaching. The religious leaders of His day hated Him because He exposed their hypocrisy, and they finally succeeded in crucifying Him. He was buried, but much to the surprise of even His disciples, the Lord Jesus rose from death as He had said. For a period of 40 days following the resurrection, He made many appearances — at one time to more than 500 people — and then He ascended to Heaven. Ten days afterward the Holy Spirit came upon His disciples, causing them to proclaim the Gospel of the living Christ with such effectiveness that countless thousands became believers in the Lord Jesus.

All of this information is recorded in the New Testament. And, do you know that this collection of books meets every accepted principle of textual and historical analysis? No less an authority than W. F. Albright, the world's foremost Biblical archaeologist, affirms that every book in the New Testament had to be written between 50 and 75 A.D., and therefore the authors were contemporaries of Jesus Christ. Do you realize that these books have the absolute right to be considered trustworthy historical documents? Do you know that the unbeliever who denies the deity of Christ and the reality of His resurrection is rejecting two of the best documented facts in history?

If you are to achieve happiness, you must believe God's declaration through Jesus Christ. A noted philosopher recently said that an atheist may be a relatively good person and look at life without losing his composure, but that he cannot be a happy man. No one can find joy in believing that all the accomplishments of human genius and labor are destined to complete extinction. God wants you to be happy, however, and to know that He loves you. In fact, He stepped into history in the person of Jesus Christ to show you what He is like and to provide for your *eternal* happiness, and He asks you to believe Him.

The faith of which the Bible speaks is not vague and indefinable. The Scriptures declare that God has eternally existed in three persons, and that He is infinitely holy as well as limitless in power and love. The Bible also makes known to man his sinfulness, and points out that only through faith in the Lord Jesus Christ can he receive forgiveness of sin.

Furthermore, the faith of the Bible is not a work through which one earns salvation or merits favor with God. It is merely the link by which the needy sinner is connected with the redemption God has provided. Many pastors are confronted by anxious people who bemoan their "weak faith," and despair because they do not think their faith is strong enough to please God. Friend, your faith may be weak, but if it has been placed in Christ, you may be sure you are saved. The Lord Jesus promised,

> Verily, verily, I say unto you, He that heareth my word, and believeth on him that sent me, hath everlasting life, and shall not come into judgment, but is passed from death unto life (John 5:24).

When you realize that salvation is all of grace, and that it is a gift received through faith, you will not be upset or feel insecure if someone tells you that you were not baptized the right way, or that you must speak in tongues before you can be saved, or that you need some special ex-

Love ✓
grateful
Do His ✓
will

perience, must keep the Sabbath, the Feast of Tabernacles, or other Old Testament observances. You will know that your faith, weak or imperfect though it may be, is placed in Jesus Christ and what He has done for you. This realization will give you spiritual security and stability.

We have seen that the faith which brings happiness is rooted in history and has intellectual content. It also involves the emotions and will. When a person believes the Gospel, he cannot help but love the Lord, be grateful to Him, and delight in doing His will. Paul wrote,

> . . . .God be thanked, that whereas ye were the servants of sin, ye have obeyed from the heart that form of doctrine which was delivered you (Romans 6:17).

The content of faith is declared in the words, "that form of doctrine which was delivered you," while the emotional and volitional aspects are expressed in the words, "ye have obeyed from the heart." True faith produces a new outlook and a changed life.

II. FORGIVENESS

The second ingredient of a happy life is the assurance of divine forgiveness. When a person believes in God and recognizes himself as a morally responsible being, he will be aware of his own sinfulness. *Emotionally Angry/edgy!*

Many people have become neurotic because they are living with deep feelings of guilt. Some psychologists would tell them they have only a guilt complex, and they must abandon the idea of a personal God who observes their every thought and act. Such advice may result in a certain freedom from the *feeling* of guilt, but the *fact* of guilt will remain. This philosophy of life ultimately leads to frustration and despair, for if there is no God to condemn sin there is no God who gives life meaning. One cannot believe in his own worth unless he acknowledges responsibility to the God who made him. For a person to be happy, he needs to know how his sin can be forgiven. Only then can he have fellowship with the Lord.

One cannot fully appreciate the teaching of the Bible regarding forgiveness unless he understands the doctrine of justification. Paul declares,

> Therefore, being justified by faith, we have peace with God through our Lord Jesus Christ,

By whom also we have access by faith into this grace
in which we stand, and rejoice in hope of the glory of
God (Romans 5:1, 2).

The Greek word translated "justified" means "to declare
righteous." It's a legal term denoting that the accused has
been acquitted of guilt and restored to a place of favor
and acceptance.

God pardons sinners on the basis of the work of the
Lord Jesus. The second person of the Trinity took upon
Himself human nature, being born of the virgin Mary. He
first lived a perfect life, then went to the cross as the
"lamb without blemish" (1 Peter 1:19), our substitute.
There He endured the "wages of sin," which is "death"
(Romans 6:23). He suffered eternal death — separation
from God — during the three hours of darkness, bearing the
wrath of God against the sin of the world. We can never
fully fathom the suffering of these hours. Nor can we understand what it meant for the Lord Jesus, having lived His
entire earthly life in perfect fellowship with the Father, to
experience that desolation of hell which caused Him to
cry, "My God, my God, why hast thou forsaken me?"
(Matthew 27:46). Only after He knew He had completely
drained the cup of suffering, and had paid the full price
for sin, did He say, "It is finished" (John 19:30), allowing
Himself to die physically with the triumphant cry, "Father,
into thy hands I commend my spirit" (Luke 23:46). Three
days later He arose from the dead, and Paul declares that
it was "for our justification" (Romans 4:25).

Do you understand the truth that by this one sacrifice
our Lord Jesus satisfied once for all the righteous demands
of a holy God?

But this man, after he had offered one sacrifice for sins
forever, sat down on the right hand of God (Hebrews
10:12).

When you believe that Jesus Christ died for your sins,
you are justified — forgiven, and accepted by God.

If you wonder how a weak, blundering, imperfect individual like yourself can expect to enter Heaven immediately upon death, remember what the Lord Jesus has done
for you. Your faith may be weak, but it has linked you to
Christ. There is nothing left for you to pay, no works for

The Basis of a Happy Life

15

you to perform, no worthiness for you to attain. The death of Jesus Christ is God's complete provision for you. Even when you sin, you do not lose your new position in Christ. The joy of communion with God will be restored if you confess your sin; and the way is always open.

> If we confess our sins, he is faithful and just to forgive us our sins, and to cleanse us from all unrighteousness (1 John 1:9).

III. NEW LIFE

True happiness is attained by confident belief in a personal God, and the assurance that the guilt of sin has been removed. In the continuing process, another definite need is deliverance from the power of sin. Believers have received a new life which enables them to overcome sin, the miracle to which our Lord had reference when He said to Nicodemus,

> . . . Verily, verily, I say unto thee, Except a man be born of water and of the Spirit, he cannot enter into the kingdom of God (John 3:5).

This new birth is necessary because everyone is born with a guilty and depraved nature inherited from Adam. The seeds of selfishness and the inclination toward evil are a part of our fallen humanity, but God does not seek to improve or repair this inherited nature. Instead, He imparts new life to the one who receives Christ, and that person becomes "a new creation."

> Therefore, if any man be in Christ, he is a new creation; old things are passed away; behold, all things are become new (2 Corinthians 5:17).

The power of the new birth has been demonstrated in the lives of millions. Men and women in the grip of alcoholism, homosexuality, and every other imaginable vice have found deliverance through faith in the Lord Jesus.

Many Christians are perplexed, however, because they are still far from what they know they ought to be and desire to be. Though experiencing a growing measure of victory over sin, they are still plagued by evil thoughts and selfish desires. The hymnwriter expressed this frustration when he wrote, "Prone to wander, Lord, I feel it. Prone to leave the God I love." This continued struggle arises from the old sinful nature which remains in the believer throughout his earthly life. Paul, thirty years after his conversion, recognized the presence of his sinful self when he wrote,

> . . . I know that in me (that is, in my flesh) dwelleth no good thing. . . .
> Oh, wretched man that I am! Who shall deliver me from the body of this death? (Romans 7:18, 24).

Paul was well aware that even though he had received the new birth he could not live a victorious life in his own strength. But he was not dismayed, for he knew he could triumph over sin as he continually looked to Jesus Christ. Therefore, immediately following the question of Romans 7:24, he penned the glorious words: "I thank God through Jesus Christ, our Lord" (Romans 7:25).

Yes, thank God, you can be an overcomer. Your life, though it will never be perfect on this side of Heaven, can be marked by righteousness. Do not despair when you find you have sinned. Follow the injunction of 1 John 1:9 and confess it. If you have forsaken that sin, be assured your fellowship with God has been restored. His plan for you includes increasing victory over sin here, and eventual deliverance from its very presence in Heaven.

God wants you to be happy. He has told you He loves you, and has given you good reason to believe Him. He does not ask you to trust in abstract theories which arise in the minds of philosophers, nor to believe in unfounded myth. Rather, He has revealed Himself in the person of Jesus Christ. The story of our Lord's birth, His ministry, His words, His death, His resurrection, and His ascension into Heaven are recorded in documents which meet every requirement for dependability and trustworthiness. When you believe the message of the Bible, you will have the assurance that God loves you, that your sins have been forgiven, and that you are indeed a child of God. This means His love for you will never change, and everything that comes into your life is part of His plan for your eternal welfare. Believe this and you will be on the road to true happiness.

2

PHYSICAL HINDRANCES TO A HAPPY LIFE

Most people who ask us for counseling are seeking spiritual help, and often their problems are caused by physical factors. Some suffer periods of deep depression because of poor health or crippling handicaps, and others are disturbed because in their affliction they feel a spirit of rebellion against God. They find it hard to believe that a person experiencing physical distress or limitation can be truly happy. We cannot fully understand the anguish of those who suffer constant pain or must live a very restricted life, and we should not be harsh in judging them. The fact is, however, that many people with severely impaired health have found pleasure and satisfaction in life. Pastors have often spoken of parishioners who were blind, or ill with terminal cancer, or bedridden with a chronic disease, but nevertheless were radiant with true happiness.

Often afflicted Christians, deeply moved when they hear about godly saints triumphing over serious bodily pain or handicaps, long for the same victorious attitude. Indeed, some who truly know the Lord go through times of severe despondency and discouragement. This is not because of a lack of provision on God's part, however, for He is ready to give every sufferer the needed grace to rise above affliction.

Two Biblical exhortations are addressed to the believer who is enduring physical trials. He must (1) exercise his faith, and (2) actively practice love.

I. Exercise Faith

To be a happy person, the suffering child of God must first exercise faith in God. True, some people without faith are able stoically to accept their lot without complaining or showing signs of weakness, and a few unusual individuals actually rise above their afflictions through actively helping others. But only a Christian can rejoice in the confidence that he has a Heavenly Father who loves him. Only a believer can possess the assurance that someday he will be delivered from his present plight to enter a glorious eternity of perfection and happiness. To enjoy these Christian certainties the child of God must exercise his faith, accepting what the Bible says about suffering and obeying its exhortations.

The Bible declares that the Lord has a loving purpose in permitting trial and testing, and assures us that His plans will be realized. He is all-powerful, and not a mere spectator standing by helplessly as you languish in pain. He freely imparts to you His power. Moreover, He is too wise to make mistakes and too good to be cruel. You must begin to exercise your faith by believing that God sees your suffering from the perspective of infinite wisdom, and realize that He develops character through affliction — producing purity, patience, compassion, and childlike trust in Himself.

Suffering is a purifying factor in the lives of God's children, even as fire removes alloys from the raw ore in the production of fine steel, pure gold, or sterling silver. Job, the classic example of a godly man who endured grievous distress of body and mind, recognized this refining purpose when he said,

> . . . he knoweth the way that I take; when he hath tested me, I shall come forth as gold (Job 23:10).

Commenting on this passage of Scripture, my father once wrote,

> It is said that if a bar of steel worth $5 were made into ordinary horseshoes, it would be worth $10. If the same steel were manufactured into needles, the value would rise to $350, but if it were made into delicate springs for expensive watches, it would be worth $250,000. Most of the increase in value lies in the labor, giving it temper, cutting it to proper size, and passing it through the heat again and again. It must be hammered and manipulated, beaten and pounded, finished and polished until finally ready for its delicate task.

This parable has an application for every child of God. We must realize that God expends His efforts only on that which gives promise of having value. We need the clouds, the dark days, the storms and the rain just as much as we need the sunshine; and God, who is molding our lives, seeking to make us like unto the Lord Jesus Christ, is the One who knows what is best for us. (M. R. De Haan, *The Ministry of Suffering*, p. 18.)

We must remind ourselves that God is perfect in wisdom and power, and say with Job, "He knoweth the way that I take." God knows what He is doing, and what He does is right. If we consciously trust Him, we will be able to say with the patriarch, "When he hath tested me, I shall come forth as gold."

Physical suffering is also a means through which God develops patience. Paul declares that as Christians "we glory in tribulations also, knowing that tribulation worketh patience" (Romans 5:3). This is more than mere passive endurance, for it is the attitude which actively overcomes difficulty. The song writer Benjamin Schmolck manifested New Testament patience when, after two of his children were burned to death, and he himself had been stricken with paralysis which led to his becoming an invalid and blind, he was able to write:

> My Jesus as Thou wilt:
> O may Thy will be mine.
> Into Thy hand of love
> I would my all resign.
> Through sorrow or through joy,
> Conduct me as Thine own,
> And help me still to say,
> "My Lord, Thy will be done."

Many of God's children have testified that out of pain and crippling disability they have extracted an inner peace and serenity never before experienced. This is the patience of which Paul speaks — a sweet consciousness of God's presence that nothing can destroy.

Affliction has value as well in leading people to become compassionate. Paul praised the God of all comfort,

> Who comforteth us in all our tribulation, that we may be able to comfort them who are in any trouble, by the

comfort with which we ourselves are comforted of God (2 Corinthians 1:4).

We often have little sympathy for others until we experience tribulation ourselves. Some never learn to intercede with genuine compassion for the multitudes who suffer from hunger or dreaded diseases until they themselves undergo physical trials. If our affliction gives us true concern and enables us to pray effectively, it is certainly worth whatever discomfort we might endure.

Pain, blindness, or disease may also be necessary to teach us to be humbly dependent upon God. Writing about the months during which the results of a heart attack greatly curtailed his ministry, my father said that Isaiah 30:15 was a source of great spiritual help to him. A vigorous and enterprising person by nature, he learned simply to wait upon the Lord. The verse reads,

> . . . In returning and rest shall ye be saved; in quietness and in confidence shall be your strength . . . (Isaiah 30:15).

God told the Israelites they would be delivered from their desperate situation if they would rest in confidence upon Him instead of seeking alliances with heathen neighbors. Like the people of Israel, we have a tendency to trust in our own strength or to consult human friends rather than humbly turning to God. Sometimes we must reach the place where our fellow men are no longer able to help us before we learn to rely wholly upon Him. A former Radio Bible Class member, who since has gone to be with the Lord, declared that major surgery for a malignant condition proved to be the greatest experience of her life, because it taught her how to trust God and live in fellowship with Him.

Yes, God afflicts us to correct us and draw us close to Himself. He loves us, and works to purify us, teaching us lessons in patience, compassion, and faith. I pray that the Holy Spirit will use what I have written in this chapter to show you the way to be happy in suffering. The infinitely wise, loving, and powerful God revealed in the Bible always has a gracious purpose in our affliction, working all things to our eventual good.

We exercise our faith not only in believing what the Bible

says about suffering, but also in obeying the practical exhortations it contains. We will consider two of these injunctions — "Count it all joy when ye fall into various trials" (James 1:2), and, "My son, despise not thou the chastening of the Lord" (Hebrews 12:5).

James was addressing believers enduring persecution for their faith when he said, "Count it all joy when ye fall into various trials." His words have a definite application to every handicapped or suffering person. Of course, James didn't expect believers to jump up and down in glee because of affliction, but he did expect that they could find occasion for joy in their suffering. They were to reflect upon what it could do for the development of their character and the deepening of their Christian experience.

Christian friend, consider what God has done to save you, and meditate upon the greatness of His wisdom, power, and love. Then draw the logical conclusion that God loves you, and that everything will work out for your eternal welfare. He has proven His love by sending Christ to die for your sins. Believe this, and don't become rebellious; don't complain that the Lord hasn't been fair to you. Think of the multitudes who live without faith in a loving Heavenly Father, and who have absolutely no hope as they contemplate death and eternity. Exercise your faith in God, and you will experience a deep inner joy even though at times you may shed tears of pain or disappointment. You will find that life is still worth living. The periods of depression will always be made less severe by your faith, and God's grace will lift you up again and again. You will find many reasons for joy and optimism.

The writer of Hebrews reminds us that we must not "despise" the chastening of our Heavenly Father. We often need correction, and God does for us exactly what a good earthly father does when his children need to be disciplined. He declares:

> Now no chastening for the present seemeth to be joyous, but grievous; nevertheless, afterward it yieldeth the peaceable fruit of righteousness unto them who are exercised by it (Hebrews 12:11).

Children never appreciate discipline at the time it is being administered. Its value is seen later. Thus it is in our relationship to our Heavenly Father. We may not always understand God's ways, but in faith we yield to Him, neither rebelling against Him nor languishing in despair. Again, this requires an exercise of faith on our part, but God has given us abundant reason to believe Him, and to have absolute confidence in His wisdom, love, and power.

II. PRACTICE LOVE

The way to happiness in suffering is not only to be found in the exercising of faith, but also in the practicing of love. One who is cut off from the normal activities of healthy people often feels "left out." He soon thinks people do not care, begins to take a low view of himself, and finally even doubts God's love for him. Such a person finds it hard to talk about the Christian life. He doesn't have the proper estimate of himself as the object of God's care, cannot love people who seem to be neglecting him, and doesn't know how he possibly could love a God who has been so slow to answer his prayers. He is tempted to engage in self-pity and say, "How can I love God when He doesn't show any love for me? How can I love people when they don't care for me? I am a nuisance to others, and might as well be dead."

Dear afflicted child of God, remember that the Lord has already proved His love for you. Jesus declared that we should love even those who hate us, and commanded us to possess a three-directional love — to God, to others, and to self. The Lord Jesus said,

> . . . Thou shalt love the Lord, thy God, with all thy heart, and with all thy soul, and with all thy mind.
> This is the first and great commandment.
> And the second is like it, Thou shalt love thy neighbor as thyself.
> On these two commandments hang all the law and the prophets (Matthew 22:37-40).

The Lord did not make love an option. No person can be truly happy or feel that he is fulfilling his purpose in life without love for God, for others, and for self.

The problem many people face, however, is a practical one. How can I develop real love for God when my lot in life seems to be unfair? How can I love inconsiderate people? Is it possible to love myself when I feel rejected and completely unlovely? The apostle John saw this problem, and indicated the way to fulfill our Lord's command-ment. He says it is impossible to love God unless we first love the people around us.

> If a man says, I love God, and hateth his brother, he is a liar; for he that loveth not his brother, whom he hath seen, how can he love God, whom he hath not seen? (1 John 4:20).

You cannot really love God if your heart is filled with hatred toward fellow Christians. Nor can you have a proper attitude of mind toward yourself if you are resentful. Therefore, you must begin by actively practicing love to those who in one way or another are touched by your life.

Let me make a practical suggestion. If you are a member of a church, but feel the people have been neglecting you of late, ask the Lord to fill your heart with the proper spirit of love, and then you make the first move. Call your friends, and tell them that you miss them. You may even suggest that they pay you a call; or why not ask a favor of them? This will let them know that you bear no ill will. Hundreds of people want their lives to be useful, but need a gentle reminder from time to time. Actually, you will be doing them a service by giving them the opportunity to do something for you. When you begin to love people again, you will also find a change in your attitude toward God. The blessings of salvation and the assurance of His presence will cause you to respond in love to the Lord. You will be fulfilling the first commandment: to love God with all your heart, soul, mind, and strength. Your prayers will become expressions of praise and thanksgiving. Strangely enough, you will also begin to view yourself in a different manner. Remember, God wants you to love yourself, for He told you to love your neighbors as *yourself*. You will see once again that you are indeed a child of God, and are destined for a glorious eternity. When this new outlook becomes a reality in your life, you will find yourself a completely transformed person.

3

THE EMOTIONS AND A HAPPY LIFE

Christians are often controlled by their emotions far more than by their thoughts, and therefore they alternate between heights of joy and depths of despair. This may be true of you, and you wonder how you may be a better example of God's grace and strength. You cannot be really happy as long as you have so many emotional ups and downs. You realize you are hurting your testimony for Christ by your failure to display serenity and joy in adverse circumstances. Perhaps you have tried Bible reading and prayer, but somehow you haven't found the help you need. It may be that you have become impatient with the well-meaning Christian friends who gave you this formula as the cure for all your spiritual and emotional ills. If you are shy, nervous, irritable, and uncertain of yourself, you face many difficulties the outgoing and likable person doesn't encounter, but God has made provision for you to live a satisfying and rewarding life.

In this chapter we will carefully consider the emotional life of the believer. We will recognize that it has been affected by sin, that its problems are universal, and that God will enable us to overcome doubts, fears, and periods of depression.

I. THE EMOTIONS AFFECTED BY SIN

God has made us with the capacity to love and to hate, to be joyful and sorrowful, to be elated or depressed. These feelings are necessary for our completeness as persons. What would life be like if we were unable to love, or if we could never experience joy? But we must sadly admit that the emotional aspect of our being, which so enriches life, can also cause a great deal of distress. We should therefore understand and evaluate our emotions in the light of the Bible which clearly teaches that our affections and sensibilities are out of balance because of sin, and that every person as a sinner is subject to certain emotional difficulties. The Bible tells us how we can overcome anxiety, fear, and bitter dejection.

God made us to love Him, our fellow men, and ourselves. The Lord Jesus expressed this clearly when He said,

> . . .Thou shalt love the Lord, thy God, with all thy heart, and with all thy soul, and with all thy mind.
> This is the first and great commandment.
> And the second is like it, Thou shalt love thy neighbor as thyself.
> On these two commandments hang all the law and the prophets (Matthew 22:37-40).

Since God is absolutely holy, loving Him rules out affection for anything sinful or defiled. We are to hate sin and be completely unselfish in our attitude toward God and others. When we do this, a proper respect for ourselves will follow. But we must sadly admit that this isn't the way we are. As a sinful race, we have a natural inclination to do wrong. Even the good things we do for others are often tainted by selfishness, and our lives are marred by evil desires, envy, and pride.

Furthermore, we do not possess the perfect balance between the mind, the emotions, and the will, which marked man before the fall. These three elements of personality are never found in complete harmony. An individual with an outgoing personality may find pleasure in the company of others and appear to be quite happy, but he tends to be superficial, and is usually poorly equipped to meet life's adversities. Financial disaster, the loss of a loved one, or the news that he is suffering an incurable disease will cause such a person to collapse. On the other hand, the introvert, inclined to be quiet in the presence of others, to shun close friendships, and to engage in undue self-examination and self-criticism, must be watchful that he does not become morbid or bitter. The emotional life is in need of daily correction, and we need continual reminders of our obligation to love God above all else, and to love our neighbors as ourselves. Because we are weak and sinful beings, we stand in need of God's help if we are to experience true happiness through all the problems of life and death.

II. EMOTIONAL PROBLEMS ARE UNIVERSAL

As we continue to evaluate our emotions we must recognize that doubts, fears, and times of despondency are common to all. Even some of the outstanding Bible characters experienced emotional turmoil. Jeremiah, one of the greatest of the Old Testament prophets, often wept because of the spiritual condition of the people to whom he ministered, and once in a moment of bitterness even cursed the day of his birth. On another occasion he was so discouraged that he vowed never to preach again. John the Baptist, a man of whom our Lord said no greater had been born of woman, began to have doubts while languishing in prison, wondering if Jesus Christ were indeed the true Messiah (Matthew 11). The apostle Paul, Christ's most noble follower, many years after his conversion cried out, "Oh, wretched man that I am" (Romans 7:24). It may help you to know that you are in good company if at times you become depressed because of doubts or fears. So do not allow feelings of guilt or sadness to plunge you deeper into despair. God knows your weakness, and He understands. The Psalmist said,

> As a father pitieth his children, so the Lord pitieth them that fear him.
> For he knoweth our frame; he remembereth that we are dust (Psalm 103:13, 14).

In evaluating our emotions, we should also recognize that they are closely associated with our nervous system, which in turn is influenced by our physical condition. Glandular disturbances, extreme weariness, or the reaction to a particularly moving experience may bring about an emotional response with spiritual overtones. Genesis 14 describes the stunning victory of Abraham over a confederacy of heathen kings, and the following chapter shows him in a state of deep spiritual depression. The same thing happened to Elijah. After the dramatic contest with the priests of Baal on Mount Carmel, 1 Kings, chapters 18 and 19, and the remarkable answer to his prayer for rain, he became frightened when news reached him that Jezebel was preparing to kill him. He fled in fear and sat under a juniper tree, feeling rebellious against the Lord, and asked that he might die. Even today many of God's servants declare that after an extremely busy day of spiritual activity, they must fight a feeling of frustration and depression.

Because of the close relationship between the physical and the emotional, believers who are disturbed should have a thorough medical examination. Or perhaps they should somehow curtail their activities to avoid the exhaustion that brings on inner problems. Furthermore, after a spiritual experience of great intensity, one should be prepared for the emotional letdown which almost invariably follows.

Remember these conflicts that sap your energy and make you unhappy are common to mankind. Do not allow guilt feelings to deepen your problem. Comfort yourself in the realization that some of the finest saints had similar trials, and that they were able to emerge victorious. Take whatever steps are necessary in medical treatment or a reduced schedule to eliminate the misgivings and apprehensions that seem to rise when you are not feeling well, or if your body and mind have been overtaxed. God desires you to be happy, and wants your life to be rich and rewarding.

III. EMOTIONAL HEALTH ATTAINABLE

No person should think that his nervous condition is such that he is doomed to a life of unhappiness. The Lord will enable you to live victoriously. If you are undergoing emotional or spiritual problems you must do two things as you read your Bible and pray: (1) remind yourself of God's faithfulness, and (2) concentrate on the great redemptive facts recorded in the Word of God.

Instead of bemoaning your doubts and fears, driving yourself deeper into depression, you should take a positive attitude and talk to yourself. This sounds like strange advice, but it is exactly what the author of Psalm 42 did when he was in a state of despondency. He said,

> Why art thou cast down, O my soul? And why art thou disquieted within me? Hope thou in God; for I shall yet praise him, who is the health of my countenance, and my God (Psalm 42:11).

The Psalmist was apparently unable to join with others in the public worship of the temple, and ruthless enemies were making life miserable for him. He was discouraged, but he did not remain so. He reminded himself of God's love, His power, and His gracious purpose, and it gave him the emotional lift he needed.

Paul was in prison awaiting execution when he wrote his second letter to Timothy. This young man was probably gripped by a spirit of fear as he thought of Paul's death and the future of the Christian church. The apostle gently reprimanded him, and reminded him of the gracious provisions God had made for His children.

> For God hath not given us the spirit of fear, but of power, and of love, and of a sound mind (2 Timothy 1:7).

Do not be afraid, for God has given you the Holy Spirit, who is the Spirit of power. You may be weak and timid by nature, but His presence will enable you to fulfill every task God calls you to do, and give you strength to meet the trials and temptations that will come your way.

Controlled by God's Spirit, you will also be able to love with the kind of love He has manifested to you. Your fear of failure stems from your self-love and self-concern. The Lord has given you the Holy Spirit to produce in you an unselfish love for God and others, a spiritual characteristic essential to real happiness.

Then, too, the indwelling Spirit of God bestows upon believers "a sound mind." This means that every Christian has the gift of self-control, discipline, and discriminative judgment. If you obey the Lord and trust Him, you will see things in their proper perspective, and be able to evaluate them as they really are. This eternal outlook will keep your emotions in their proper place.

Dark clouds of apprehension need not mar your present days. You can be happy in the assurance that you have been given the Holy Spirit, and that His coming into your life has brought the three desperately needed graces — power, love, and a sound mind.

Do not allow your emotions to control your life. Contemplate the great truths of the Scriptures concerning God, and talk to your own soul. Remind yourself that God is in control of your life, that He has proven His love for you by giving Jesus Christ to be your Savior, and that He hasn't changed. Why should you be discouraged when you have a Heavenly Father who has always met your needs in the past, and has promised to see you safely to glory?

Encourage yourself with the reminder that thousands of God's children have been able to face indescribable hardships and bitter persecutions without doubting God's goodness or complaining about their lot in life. They found strength in the realization that "the sufferings of this present time are not worthy to be compared with the glory which shall be revealed in us" (Romans 8:18). Tell yourself that you too may rest upon this same assurance, and that the God who gave grace and strength to others will also meet your need. Yes, the art of talking to oneself should be developed by every Christian. The Psalmist did, and so should you.

You must also focus your thoughts upon the great redemptive facts recorded in the Bible. The Lord Jesus actually lived upon this earth, died, rose from the grave, instructed His disciples, and then ascended into Heaven. These things really happened, and the Bible gives us both their history and their significance. If you desire spiritual health you must base your assurance of salvation upon these solid truths, not upon your variable and unpredictable emotions.

The late F. B. Meyer is usually credited with a fine illustration depicting the proper place of the emotions in the believer's life. He speaks of three soldiers to whom he gives the names "Fact," "Faith," and "Feeling." He points out that these three military men must always march in the proper order. "Fact" must take the lead, with "Faith" in second place, and "Feeling" must follow the other two. "Faith" must always look forward to "Fact," never glancing back to see how "Feeling" is coming along. If "Faith" does look back, he stumbles, failing to keep step with "Fact." The application to the Christian life is obvious: our *faith* must rest upon the great redemptive *facts* of the Scriptures. When *faith* does this, it is strong and unwavering, but when it begins to be dependent upon *feelings,* looking to the changeable emotions, it will waver and become ineffective. The next time doubts begin to arise in your heart and you feel despondent, exercise the faith God has given you. Think about all that is yours in Him. Remind yourself that the New Testament books meet every demand to be recognized as trustworthy historical documents, and that they are true. Center your thoughts upon what God has done to make Himself known to you, and to save you. Ask God to strengthen your faith.

True, you may not always *feel* saved, but remember that your salvation is not based upon your feelings. It is grounded upon the fact of what God has done for you. The realization of this will enable you to overcome your anxieties, and with the Psalmist you will be able to say, "I shall yet praise him, who is the health of my countenance, and my God" (Psalm 42:11). Emotional disturbances need not rob you of happiness. You can live above the faltering and fearful attitude which would deprive you of inner peace and joy.

4

GUILT FEELINGS AND A HAPPY LIFE

The minister of the Gospel who is sensitive to the spiritual needs of his people will spend much time in prayer asking the Holy Spirit to apply his sermons to the heart of each individual. Some of his listeners, seeking superficial delight in worldly pleasures, are unconcerned about the spiritual quality of their lives, and must be jolted by stern warning. Others, however, are burdened by a deep sense of guilt, and need words of comfort and healing, for their attitude of self-condemnation is a devastating force in their lives. Undue remorse breeds the fear of rejection by both God and fellow men. This sense of alienation results from an inability to receive spiritual help from either Bible reading or prayer, and a feeling of loneliness gradually develops symptoms of paranoia in the victim so that he thinks everyone is against him. He becomes furtive and secretive, and withdraws more and more from others. Unhealthy guilt feelings also render one's life ineffective, taking their toll on the body and mind by sapping the energy which could otherwise be channeled into prayer or useful work. I pray that God will make this chapter become His special word to each of you who have been unable to achieve happiness because of remorse for sins of the past or present, or a feeling of failure as you consider the wasted time and squandered opportunities of your life.

I. THE PROBLEM OF SIN

Deep guilt feelings regarding sin may stem from something done in the past, or may be the result of an unholy habit from which one has been unable to free himself. No one can be truly happy until he is released from the burden of self-condemnation.

Often the feeling of guilt relates to a particular sin or sins committed long ago. The evil word or deed seems so dreadful in nature that the troubled Christian cannot believe it is pardonable. It may have been adultery, an act of gross perversion, a lie which hurt someone deeply, or a blasphemous statement — but it cannot be forgotten. If you are having this kind of difficulty, you are being swayed by your changeable and unpredictable emotions rather than by truth. The Bible clearly declares that Jesus Christ paid the complete price for all your sins, and gives a number of specific examples of men who fell deeply but experienced the joyous assurance of forgiveness.

Jesus Christ performed a complete work of atonement for all sin on the cross. He did not allow Himself to die physically until He could say, "It is finished." He would not have said this if any transgressions could remain unforgiven.

The apostle Peter also stated the complete nature of our Lord's redemptive work when he said,

> Who his own self bore our sins in his own body on the tree, that we, being dead to sins, should live unto righteousness; by whose stripes ye were healed (1 Peter 2:24).

Peter did not say that He bore *some* of your sins on the cross, or indicate that part of your life does not come under the scope of our Lord's sacrifice. In fact, the Bible specifically announces that Christ paid the price for all the sins of the *world*, and therefore you may be certain that every sin you have ever committed has been covered by His blood.

Two outstanding men of the Bible sinned deeply, but did not allow the gravity of their evil deed to destroy their assurance of God's forgiveness. They are David and the apostle Paul.

Almost everybody knows the story of David and Bathsheba. After committing adultery with her, the king manipulated her soldier husband into a position in battle which brought about his death. David went through a period of despair and deep remorse before he confessed his transgression, for in Psalm 32 we read,

> When I kept silence, my bones became old through my roaring all the day long.

For day and night thy hand was heavy upon me . . .
(Psalm 32:3, 4).

But when he acknowledged his sin he received the assurance of God's cleansing. Paul quotes his joyous expression of gratitude in Romans 4 to illustrate the blessedness of complete forgiveness through faith.

> . . . Blessed are they whose iniquities are forgiven, and whose sins are covered.
> Blessed is the man to whom the Lord will not impute sin (Romans 4:7, 8).

If God forgave David, giving him sweet assurance and the consciousness of restored fellowship, will He do any less for you?

The apostle Paul also sinned grievously, but rejoiced in the certainty of a complete remission of all his iniquities. He never forgot that at one time he had blasphemed the name of Jesus and had violently persecuted the Church. Following his conversion to Christ, however, he never wondered whether or not God had forgiven him. In fact, he rejoiced in God's forgiving love, and, in his first letter to Timothy, after referring to himself as formerly "a blasphemer, and a persecutor, and injurious" (1 Timothy 1:13), he gratefully added,

> This is a faithful saying, and worthy of all acceptance, that Christ Jesus came into the world to save sinners, of whom I am chief.
> Nevertheless, for this cause I obtained mercy, that in me first Jesus Christ might show forth all long-suffering, for a pattern to them who should hereafter believe on him to life everlasting (1 Timothy 1:15, 16).

Paul remembered his past sin, but recognized at the same time that he was on display as a trophy of God's grace, an example of God's mercy to even the vilest sinner, bringing absolute forgiveness.

Christian friend, believe what God has said. When you act as if your particular sin is beyond forgiveness, you are implying that the Lord Jesus was wrong when He said, "It is finished." You are repudiating the testimony of David and Paul. Trust God and rejoice in the knowledge of His complete forgiveness. You are weak, yes, and at times the memory of the old sins that trouble you brings disquieting thoughts, but remember that God understands your frailty. Remind yourself that through Christ's sacrifice you are at peace with God, and rejoice in the fullness of His forgiveness.

Feelings of guilt involving sin may also concern thoughts, attitudes, or practices which you know are wrong. You desire deliverance from them, but it has not come. You have prayed, have read the Bible, and have determined not to fall again, but you are still struggling with certain sins. You have not reached the holy walk you desire. If this is a description of your life, you should (1) be thankful for this earnest desire to be holy, (2) recognize the role of Satan, and (3) comprehend the Biblical truth that you will not receive complete deliverance from sin until you reach Heaven.

You should be grateful that you desire a holy life and long for sweet communion with God. Give thanks for these aspirations He has placed within you.

It may also be comforting to know that some of your doubts and emotional distresses come from Satan, the formidable foe of God's children. Once the most glorious of all God's creatures, he fell through pride (Isaiah 14:12-17; Ezekiel 28:11-19), and now with his army of fallen spirits opposes God and His people. Paul declares,

> For we wrestle not against flesh and blood, but against principalities, against powers, against the rulers of the darkness of this world, against spiritual wickedness in high places (Ephesians 6:12).

An illustration from the period of American history when slavery was practiced shows Satan's work in the lives of those who love God. A plantation owner took his trusted slave with him as he went hunting for ducks. Standing together in a marsh, the agnostic master gently chided the black man about his religion, "I do not believe in God, and don't have nearly the emotional turmoil and distress you seem to have. The devil gives you a lot more trouble than he gives me." Just then a flock of ducks flew overhead, and the man shot at them. Two of the birds came down, one apparently lifeless, but the other wildly flapping its wings. When the slave hurried to pick up the motionless duck, the master called, "Not that one, we are sure of him." The humble believer caught the wounded bird, killed it, and with a broad smile said, "Master, I have the answer to the problem you just gave me. The reason the devil gives me such a hard time is because I have life. He leaves you alone because you are spiritually dead. It is those who have life that he troubles." Christian friend, you can be thankful that the devil counts you among his foes, for it is far better to be in God's camp than his.

The Bible also teaches that God has seen fit to withhold complete deliverance from the old sinful nature until we die. No one will be sinlessly perfect until he reaches Heaven. When Jesus said, "Be ye, therefore, perfect, even as your Father, who is in heaven, is perfect" (Matthew 5:48), He set forth the goal toward which we should strive, though He knew that in this life none of us would completely attain it. Therefore, we must realistically face our sins and shortcomings, confess them, and then believe that God does indeed forgive and cleanse.

> If we confess our sins, he is faithful and just to forgive
> us our sins, and to cleanse us from all unrighteousness
> (1 John 1:9).

We should long for holiness, but recognize that in this life we will never achieve it. Therefore God tells us to confess our sins, to make amends as much as we possibly can, and then unreservedly to trust His grace. Our failures should not throw us into a spiritual tailspin. Remember, though you cannot achieve sinlessness and unmarred happiness in this world, you will someday reach that goal. In the meantime, you may experience renewed victory over sin, and grow in the grace and knowledge of God. Your life will not be perfect, but it can be happy and satisfying.

II. THE PROBLEM OF VAIN REGRET

Another burden which hinders the life of many Christians is regret. With an ever-increasing sense of guilt over wasted time and squandered opportunities, they look back and say, "If only I had surrendered to Christ when I was younger!" For the benefit of those who are spending their time and energy mourning over past failure, I would like to make three observations: (1) It is foolish and wasteful; (2) it is paralyzing; (3) it is basically selfish.

To be morbidly preoccupied with past failure is foolish and wasteful, because the timeclock cannot be reversed.

The past cannot be recalled, and all your regrets will do nothing to correct it. The adage, "No use crying over spilled milk" makes good sense here. That we should learn lessons from the past is true, but we should not submerge ourselves in vain remorse over wasted years or lost opportunities.

This unhealthy grief is also paralyzing, for it robs one of present effectiveness. We might compare the person who spends his time grieving about the lost opportunities of the past to a singer whose talent is discovered late in his life. Suppose a vocalist, when given a chance to sing before a nationwide audience, said, "I should have been doing this for twenty years. I have perhaps ten years left to exercise my abilities, and therefore I think I will just forget about this new opportunity. I keep thinking of the twenty years that have gone by." We would say to such a person, "Man, forget about those years during which your talent was wasted. Take advantage of the opening you have now." Christian friend, do not fret over the past, but use the opportunities and talents you possess to glorify God and bring blessing to your fellow men. *Get with it!* Serve the Lord *today* with joy and zeal!

An unwholesome attitude of gloom toward the past reveals that you are still self-centered. If you really love God with all your heart, and truly love your neighbor as yourself, you will do what you can to serve the Lord and your fellow men, leaving the matter of judgment to God. Your undue concern about past failure is selfish, and undoubtedly in part stems from your desire to be highly esteemed. You should follow the example of Paul, who, though he regretted the period in his life during which he blasphemed the name of Jesus and persecuted the saints, and though he was deeply hurt by false charges and accusations made against him, did not allow these things to hinder his ministry. Writing to the Corinthian believers, he said,

> But with me it is a very small thing that I should be judged of you, or of man's judgment; yea, I judge not mine own self.
> For I know nothing against myself, yet am I not hereby justified; but he that judgeth me is the Lord (1 Corinthians 4:3, 4).

The apostle realized that what others thought of him didn't really matter, and that his own estimate of himself was also relatively unimportant. The Lord was his Judge, and therefore he was glad to give himself unstintingly to the task before him.

Remember, we easily deceive ourselves. It looks humble to mourn over the little we have done for God, but in reality this is taking an exalted view of our talents and potential. Yes, each of us is responsible to do his best for God and others, and it is as every person fills his own niche that great things are accomplished. Yet we must be aware that not one of us is indispensable, and that our contribution to the world is small. When we die, life will go on without interruption or perceptible change except for the members of our immediate family. Milton, a brilliant man who became blind at an early age, was convinced that we serve God best when we humbly bear our burdens without murmuring, for he said,

> Thousands at his bidding speed
> And post o'er land and ocean without rest:
> *They also serve who only stand and wait.*

You must realize that your relationship with God is the important thing, not the amount of money you give or the years of service you render. When you are living in fellowship with Him, you will serve Him in a spirit of unselfishness without thought of reward. The widow who gave only a mite presented her all because she loved God, not because she was seeking a return on her gift, and the Lord will richly reward her in Heaven.

Do not be occupied in vain regrets, but serve Christ today. You were saved by grace through faith, and not by works. Trust God with the matter of your rewards as well, and serve Him because you love Him and desire to do His bidding. Your life will then please Him, and that should be your greatest concern. The way of happiness is through the time-proven path of faith and obedience. If you believe God, the burden of your guilt will be lifted. If you obey Him, regulating your life in obedience with our Lord's command to love God above all, and your neighbor as yourself, you will not be plagued with vain regrets. Yes, if you will believe the Lord and obey Him, you will be happy!

5

FREEDOM FROM FEAR

True happiness is impossible for the one who lives in constant fear. Gnawing feelings of dread and anxiety distort reality, benumb the emotions, and paralyze the will. Much of the nervous tension afflicting multitudes today can be traced to fear. The effect in some people is extreme weariness and irritability because they are unable to sleep; in others, it is a desire to sleep all the time, with the long hours of slumber failing to bring the rest so desperately sought. Dark thoughts concerning the future cloud the mind, work becomes drudgery, and living yields no pleasure. Often the person cannot name anything specific of which he is afraid, but his undefined feeling of fear is largely responsible for various physical symptoms which give him great distress. He suffers indigestion, pains in the stomach, or sharp stabs in the area of his heart. He wonders if he has cancer, or if he is going to be one of those who dies suddenly from a heart attack. He may develop a throbbing headache which makes him worry about a brain tumor. Yet, whenever he undergoes a physical examination, the doctors are unable to find anything seriously wrong. The patient is not satisfied, however, for he supposes that somehow his malady has not been discovered. Surely, he feels, one cannot be so exhausted or have so much pain unless something is severely wrong!

To tell this person that his troubles are mental, and that his pain and exhaustion are not real will not solve his problem. The root of his difficulty must be uncovered. Sometimes this will require a trained psychologist or psychiatrist, but often the sufferer's deepest need is spiritual.

He must find deliverance from his unrest — the apprehension which may be either (1) the fear of failure or (2) the dread of dying.

I. THE FEAR OF FAILURE

To be labeled a failure is humiliating, and most people will do all they can to avoid it. Almost everyone wishes to be recognized or respected, and many live in continual fear that they will be unable to live up to the standards expected of them or meet emergencies that may arise. This fear of failure involves both everyday experience and matters relating to God and eternity.

Often people suffer from what is termed an "inferiority complex." They may have average intelligence or above, a good appearance, and other plus factors, but have no confidence in themselves. This sense of inadequacy causes them to worry about the future, wondering what they would do if the dire events they imagine were actually to take place. They are afraid that if certain loved ones were to die, they would be unable to face life and its problems.

Child of God, if you are plagued by these feelings, you must recognize that you are being swayed by your emotions, not by the truth. You most likely have adequate ability and intelligence, and possibly may be operating on a level far lower than necessary because you use only a fraction of the potential you have. The same is true of many people. Remember, God is your Maker, and He will not call upon you to perform a task beyond your ability, or to meet a trial for which He will not give you strength. We are assured,

> There hath no temptation taken you but such as is common to man; but God is faithful, who will not permit you to be tempted above that ye are able, but will, with the temptation, also make the way to escape, that ye may be able to bear it (1 Corinthians 10:13).

Therefore, trust your Heavenly Father, for He has proven that He loves you. Didn't Jesus declare that even the birds and lilies, who can acknowledge neither God's creative power nor His love, are fed and clothed by Him? Don't you think He will meet your needs? Trust Him to give you strength and grace.

Many believers, though well-adjusted and able to meet

the problems of everyday life with poise and equanimity, are apprehensive about spiritual failure. Perhaps you are one of them, and you are concerned because your prayer-life is not satisfying, your Bible reading a chore, your consciousness of God's presence practically nil, and your spiritual influence negligible. You certainly do not want to be in this condition when you die! You may even be afraid that sometime you will fall into deep sin or lose your faith completely.

If you are to be delivered from these fears, and find true happiness in life, the first thing you must do is concentrate upon fulfilling the purpose for which God saved you. You can do this only through obedience and the exercise of faith. You must take seriously our Lord's words when He said,

> . . . Thou shalt love the Lord, thy God, with all thy heart, and with all thy soul, and with all thy mind.
> This is the first and great commandment.
> And the second is like it, Thou shalt love thy neighbor as thyself (Matthew 22:37-39).

In an earlier chapter we pointed out that one cannot magically conjure up love for God. It must be developed through obedience and a walk of fellowship with the Lord. Therefore, in the light of John's declaration that one cannot love God who is invisible if he is unable to love men who are tangible (1 John 4:20), you must direct your attention away from yourself to others. When you do good for your fellow men, seeking their true welfare, you will learn to love them, and you will begin to pray for them. This unselfish prayer will bring you into communion with God, and your heart will grow warm toward Him. Your prayer-life will be transformed, the Bible will become a delight, God's presence will be real, and your life will be influential for His glory.

If you are one of those persons who is afraid of spiritual failure because you have a low view of your ability to serve God, or doubt your strength to withstand temptation, remember that God knows your limitations and He doesn't expect anything you are incapable of doing. The Lord will reward on the basis of faithfulness. Many a person who has never led in public prayer, taught a Sunday school class, or preached a sermon will receive God's rich praise. Be faithful, and rest assured that He will not rebuke you because your talents were few. His approval of your dedicated service may exceed that of some whose accomplishments on earth seemed much greater than yours.

If you are afraid of succumbing to temptation or faltering under trial, let me remind you that God will graciously give you the strength you need for every test. We have already made reference to 1 Corinthians 10:13, where God promises never to test us beyond our capacity. Do not bring needless apprehension into your life by imagining trials which may never materialize. For example, do not worry about your strength to bear dreadful persecution in the event of a communist takeover. And, when you read of the experiences of others, do not make yourself miserable by supposing that you will be called upon to endure a similar trial. John Bunyan was in prison for preaching the Gospel, and was greatly distressed when, through the prison bars, he saw his blind daughter selling shoelaces on the street to help keep his family alive. But he received grace, and was able to produce helpful and lasting Christian literature during that dreadful time. Now, you most likely will never be called upon to pass through such an ordeal. But if it should come, you will receive supernatural grace even as Bunyan did. Do not envision the worst possible situation, and then worry about your ability to go through it with strength and confidence. The Lord Jesus told us, "Sufficient unto the day is its own evil" (Matthew 6:34).

II. Fear of Death

The fear of death is common to all mankind. Some people are able to push the thought of dying out of their minds, but every person is instinctively afraid of it. Even animals have a biological urge to live, and fight tenaciously to maintain life for themselves and their young. Their relationship to death is far different from that of humans, however, for animals are unable to contemplate what death means, and know nothing of a yearning for immortality. The human race dreads death, and longs for life beyond the grave. True, some people declare that they have no desire to continue existence in another world, but they can say this only at certain times. They cannot think like this when a loved one passes away.

Many unhappy people live in the grip of a paradoxical

attitude toward death. They are afraid of it, and yet long for it. Sometimes they contemplate suicide, but are restrained by a fear of what may lie beyond, or by concern for their loved ones, or by a vague feeling that suicide is evil. They are tired of living but afraid of dying. Shakespeare expressed this inner conflict when he wrote:

> To die, to sleep;
> To sleep: perchance to dream: ay, there's the rub;
> For in that sleep of death what dreams may come.

The Christian should have neither a fear of death nor a morbid longing for it. He should be able to talk about dying with freedom and without dread. He should be grateful for life upon earth, joyously anticipate the glory of Heaven, and be perfectly content to wait for God's time.

The Bible teaches us that we die because sin has entered the human race, and we have therefore a natural aversion to dying. Paul sums it up by saying, "For the wages of sin is death" (Romans 6:23). The Word of God further declares that Jesus Christ took the sting out of death, and that those who trust Him can be delivered from its fear. The writer of Hebrews declared that Jesus Christ took upon Himself our humanity and went to the cross "that through death he might destroy him that had the power of death, that is, the devil, and deliver them who, through fear of death, were all their lifetime subject to bondage" (Hebrews 2:14, 15).

We need not to be afraid of dying, for Jesus Christ has destroyed death's power. He settled the sin question, when, as our Substitute, He first endured the agony of hell on the cross, and then died physically. He demonstrated His power over death by His resurrection. The apostles, to whom the risen Christ made many appearances before He ascended to Heaven, went everywhere proclaiming that He was alive, and said that the Lord's resurrection was God's pledge that all who believe shall someday at Christ's return receive glorified bodies. No wonder their preaching transformed the Roman world of the first century!

God also revealed that the period between death and resurrection is one of blessedness in the presence of Christ. Therefore Paul could say that absence from the body means presence with the Lord (2 Corinthians 5:6-8), and he

Freedom From Fear

43

affirmed, "For to me to live is Christ, and to die is gain" (Philippians 1:21). He could shout in triumph concerning the resurrection, "O death, where is thy sting? O grave, where is thy victory?" (1 Corinthians 15:55).

The living Christ took the sting from death by paying its price, and won a glorious victory over it by His resurrection. Therefore, we are assured that through Him we possess everlasting life. For a believer, death means the entrance into a larger life, a better place where God's presence gleams more radiantly. When we die we immediately attain sinlessness, and we are delivered from everything evil, defiling, depressing, or sad. We who know Christ should often speak of the glory that awaits us, and talk of death freely without feeling the subject is morbid. Christians of former generations often called their loved ones together when death was imminent, calmly gave final instructions, bade a fond farewell, and expressed confidence in the glorious reunion "over there."

Some people, although they know Christ and are assured of entrance into Heaven, still fear "passing through the valley." They need not dread the experience of dying. People in terminal illness often appear to be suffering greatly, but in reality they are not conscious of distress. This is a medical fact which few question. Furthermore, a sweet peace floods the soul of the believer as the hour of death approaches. A lady told one of the members of the Radio Bible Class staff that her mother, who had lived in morbid fear of her deathbed, looked up at her husband just before leaving this world and said, "So this is dying. It's easy. Just think, all my life I have been afraid for no good reason!" Christian friend, why should you be afraid to die? Your Savior has promised never to leave you nor forsake you. He has paid the price for your sins and defeated death's sting. He rose from the grave, overcoming its power. You need not allow the inevitability of your death to be a shadow over your life, robbing you of happiness. Be thankful for every day of living on earth, but reflect often upon the Home that awaits you, rejoicing that your journey from earth to Heaven will not be difficult.

Every year thousands of people in hopelessness and despair commit suicide. Those who take this step are seldom, if ever, in control of all their faculties, and therefore we should not judge them too harshly. We should never speak of suicide as if it were the unpardonable sin. Nevertheless it is a major tragedy, and we must seek to help the person who is obsessed with taking his own life. Do not make the mistake of thinking that one who threatens self-destruction will not go through with it. He should be allowed to talk about his feelings, and should be given every encouragement to go on living.

If you have been tempted to bring about your own end, let me remind you that this will not really solve anything. As tenderly as I can, I would like to tell you it is a cowardly act, indicating that you are afraid to face life. It is selfish, for it shows a lack of concern for the loved ones who will be left. It is presumptuous, for the person who decides to take his own life is denying God's wisdom. It overlooks the love of God for man, and His provision for living victoriously every day. If you are contemplating suicide, take your Bible and read from the third chapter of Ecclesiastes:

> To every thing there is a season, and a time to every purpose under the heaven:
> A time to be born, and a time to die. . . .
> He hath made every thing beautiful in its time; also he hath set the world [i.e. eternity] in their heart . . . (Ecclesiastes 3:1, 2, 11).

God has a beautiful plan for every believer, and in it He has His own time for one to be born and to die. When a birth is forced prematurely, life is destroyed before it really begins, and when one brings on death by his own hand he denies its beauty and eternal significance. God has made it clear that through suicide one cannot escape from reality, for the spirit continues and the resurrection is coming. He therefore wants us to place our lives in His hands, and to live joyously in fellowship with Him until the day He calls us home.

Christian friend, the Lord loves you and desires your happiness. Exercise your faith. Trust Him and obey Him. If you learn to love God above all, and your neighbor as yourself, you will find life rich and meaningful. You will then be able to live every day in the awareness of the Lord's presence, and you will look forward with steadfast hope. Yes, you can be truly happy!

Part II

HAPPINESS IN A
CHANGING WORLD

6

THE SPIRITUAL VACUUM

The songwriter's words "The times, they are a'changin,'" are so obviously true that it seems trite to repeat them. Older people who glance at the book and magazine counters can recall a time when a man who wanted to sell dirty books or pictures had to do it secretly because he would be prosecuted if caught. They notice that many young people openly ridicule the old standards and see no reason to live up to the moral code taught in the Bible. Most adults can remember days when almost everyone accepted the meaning of the injunction, "be good," and believed it to be proper even if they did not practice it.

The memory of an almost universal attitude of abhorrence toward homosexuality is fresh in the minds of the middle-aged people of this generation, but today perversion is either looked upon lightly, or openly advocated. Time was when criminals were considered enemies of society, for they had broken the law and deserved to be punished. Today behavioristic psychologists tell us that acts of stealing, murder, or rape are merely the products of body chemistry or unfortunate environmental conditions, and that those who commit them are not to be blamed for their crimes. Thieves and hoodlums are referred to merely as underprivileged people, though most of them have enjoyed material blessings undreamed of by their forbears. Young men wielding switchblade knives and bicycle chains are defended as innocent victims of our cruel society. No wonder our present era is often called "the twisted age"!

Have these changes in society made people happier today than they were years ago? Of course not! Most of the youth are frustrated and take a dim view of the future. They are victims of a godless philosophy of life which has captured the mind of modern man. The general teaching throughout the universities is that man is the product of impersonal force plus time and change, an accident of nature having no significance, no purpose, no meaning, and no eternal conscious destiny. Young people who accept this philosophy of life are frustrated. They have despaired of finding any true values, and their conduct reflects their attitude. The mere fact that everything is changing rapidly does not account for the unhappiness of multitudes, however; it is a fact that most people are living in a spiritual vacuum. Mankind has departed from God, has rejected absolute standards of conduct, and has accepted an approach to life which has aptly been named a "philosophy of despair."

I. Departure From God

A large segment of our society has abandoned God. In fact, the denial of God's existence is not unusual today. Even theologians speak of the death of God, meaning by that phrase that they do not believe in a living God as revealed in the Bible. Many scientists, accepting the theory of naturalistic evolution, teach that men no longer need to think of a God. They postulate neatly spun theories of how things came into being, rejecting the personal God of the Christian faith.

When men deny the existence of God they willfully reject the testimony of the created world. Therefore they are responsible for their unbelief and guilty before God. Paul declares,

> For the wrath of God is revealed from heaven against all ungodliness and unrighteousness of men, who hold the truth in unrighteousness,
> Because that which may be known of God is manifest in them; for God hath shown it unto them.
> For the invisible things of him from the creation of the world are clearly seen, being understood by the things that are made, even his eternal power and Godhead, so that they are without excuse (Romans 1:18, 19, 20).

Nature testifies of God, for it gives evidence of having a designer and creator. The Bible says that men "hold the truth in unrighteousness." This expression may mean that they hinder, hold down, or suppress the truth that comes to them through the created world. Another possible interpretation of the words, "to hold the truth in unrighteousness," is that they hold as much of the truth as they think they need, but in their wickedness and rebellion against God do not accept the full implications of His existence for their daily living. Many will admit that some kind of intelligence is behind the universe, but they reject the idea of a personal God who has set moral standards and demands obedience to them. In either case, whether men suppress the truth that comes to them in nature or refuse to accept the full implications of it, the Lord holds them responsible.

The first chapter of Romans elaborates upon the deliberate character of man's ignorance. The knowledge of God is available to men, but they "do not like to retain God in their knowledge" (v. 28). Humanity has always preferred to establish its own religious systems, embracing wicked forms of idolatry and falling into the deepest depravity imaginable. Abundant evidence from archaeology shows that man did not gradually evolve from lower religious concepts to a high monotheism. On the contrary, the earliest men were monotheists, but they rejected the revelation God gave of Himself, and gradually devised polytheistic religious systems and began to worship idols. Therefore the world stands morally responsible before God, and the human race in its natural condition stands under condemnation.

When men no longer believe in God, they reject not only the testimony of the natural world about them, but also the voice that speaks within their own being. Every man knows that his thought life sets him apart from the animal. He cannot help but reflect upon death and eternity. He possesses an instinctive knowledge of right and wrong. Paul points this out saying,

> For when the Gentiles, who have not the law, do by nature the things contained in the law, these, having not the law, are a law unto themselves;
> Who show the work of the law written in their hearts, their conscience also bearing witness, and their thoughts the meanwhile accusing or else excusing one another (Romans 2:14, 15).

Anthropologists report that studies of primitive people of the past and present show that every society, however undeveloped, gives evidence of acquaintance with moral and spiritual concepts. We may therefore properly consider every philosophical or scientific system which denies the supernatural as being a *departure* from God. Modern thought in general is dominated by those who have *refused* to believe in God, and the immorality and turbulence of our times are the result.

II. DENIAL OF STANDARDS

Society today has also rejected certain standards which were generally accepted a few generations ago. This is because men have rejected God. Belief in the Lord as He is revealed in the Bible is not merely a speculative problem of little practical importance. It involves all of life, both for society and the individual.

Christians believe in a personal God who created all things, and look upon the universe as both real and understandable. In other words, we believe that an intelligent and reasonable God created a world which we can study and to a great extent understand. Early scientists like Copernicus, Bacon, Galileo, and Newton believed in God, and held that the world He created is reasonable, orderly, and reflects both a divine plan and purpose. They were convinced that through the exercise of his intelligence man could fulfill to some extent, though now a sinful, fallen creature, God's charge to subdue the earth and exercise dominion over it (see Genesis 1:26). They declared that the Lord had established natural laws of cause and effect which could be depended upon, and that man, an intelligent personality created in the image and likeness of God, by discovering these laws could either utilize them or interrupt their flow to accomplish certain ends. For example, man has utilized natural laws in the production of electricity, and interrupts the flow of natural law whenever he overcomes the pull of gravity and sends a plane aloft.

The early scientists believed that God the Creator stands distinct from and above the laws of the universe He has made, and that man as His special creation is also observedly different from the plant and animal world.

Our twentieth century, however, has been marked by an almost universal acceptance of the theory of naturalistic evolution. This hypothesis, built upon circumstantial evidence and a great deal of imagination, sets forth a concept of life from the standpoint of reason. This system of thought, called rationalism, begins with man and seeks to explain everything without going beyond him and his world. However, all efforts of man to present a unified system of thought without a basic belief in God has far-reaching consequences. If there be no personal God, then the universe as we know it is simply the product of impersonal force plus time plus chance. If one accepts this theory, the concept of man as a personal being must also be abandoned.

It is impossible to conceive of a personality being produced by impersonal force. Therefore, today many non-Christian intellectuals believe that man is not truly a person in the full sense of the word. They consider him to be an unexplainable element in this chance-produced world, and deny the reality of man's freedom to make choices. They insist that what he does and thinks is completely under the control of chemical processes within his body or psychological factors to which he has been subjected. They therefore believe that man has no real significance, and that his life and being are without purpose. Thus man is really not essentially different from the rock he removes from his garden, the plants he raises there, or the birds and rodents he tries to keep out of it. No wonder the world is so filled with unhappy people. Mankind cannot live in a spiritual vacuum which reduces him to a meaningless blob.

A departure from God influences not only one's concept of man's worth and significance, but also his attitude toward moral conduct. If no God exists, no divinely established principles for the regulation of human conduct are possible. As a result, each individual must work out his own moral system, and society is responsible to establish rules for self-preservation and the common good. Murder would be forbidden, not because it is intrinsically wrong, but because such a law would be necessary for the betterment of humanity. The criteria for right and wrong would therefore not be the revealed principles and absolute standards given by God, but the arbitrary regulations decided upon by society. These might change from generation to generation.

An atheistic view of life also removes the concept of individual responsibility for crime. The rapist or murderer, according to naturalistic evolutionists, did not deliberately choose to commit his crime but was driven to it by a chemical or psychological force beyond his control. He is a victim of either heredity or his present environment, not a violator of the laws of God. Therefore many voices today insist that criminals need treatment and therapy, not punishment. In total, the modern world denies absolute standards of conduct, and looks upon man merely as a machine. This concept of man and morality may be of some comfort to people whose conduct is wicked, immoral, or anti-social, but cannot produce happiness or true satisfaction.

III. The Philosophy of Despair

The word "despair," often used in connection with twentieth-century man, describes his response to the conclusion that he is an insignificant and meaningless creature who is programmed like a computer, possessing no freedom and making no moral choices. For those who think deeply, the logical consequence of the denial of God gives rise to inner tension. A man may say he does not believe he is anything more than a machine, and affirm that terms like love are words without real meaning. But unless he is completely devoid of human sensitivity, he cannot maintain his philosophy when he looks upon his wife and children. He may say that a quality like love does not really exist, but he cannot practice this definition in real life. He finds himself in conflict, and must search for an avenue of deliverance from the despair brought about by his departure from God.

Many philosophers and theologians have turned to a system of thought called existentialism. They say that we must rationally accept the fact that life is meaningless, even absurd, but that somehow, through a non-rational feeling or act, we can gain an experience that will help us. Some secular existentialists speak vaguely of "authenticating ourselves," while the religious existentialists speak of a "salvation," but do not, will not, and cannot define it. Many people seek to "authenticate themselves" through pornographic literature and grossly immoral conduct. Others try to gain an experience through psychedelic music or the use of drugs. Yet, the men and women who think carefully about the implications of their denial of the supernatural are experiencing deep inner wretchedness.

Among those who refuse to face the logical conclusions of their unbelief, are people for whom the despair of a meaningless life has taken a slightly different turn. Many simply put aside thoughts of death and eternity as much as possible and give themselves to the pursuit of pleasure. We have all become acquainted with the desperado, the lawless man with a price on his head who lives recklessly because he feels he has nothing to lose except his own worthless life. The popular maxim, "eat, drink, and be merry for tomorrow we die," has become a way of life for many such people. However, even they undoubtedly experience moments of dread as they contemplate their dismal future.

The Christian attitude toward the unbelieving world must be that of compassion. Rather than ridiculing the hippies, pornographic writers, abstract artists, and wild musicians, we should pray earnestly for them. Somehow we must communicate to them the fact that God exists, that He has revealed Himself, that He can be known, and that salvation is available through Jesus Christ. They must be able to see in us a radiant joy that is constant and steadfast even in this changing world. They must see that the Gospel is the only hope for a despairing world. They must be made to realize that the Lord Jesus is ready, willing, and able to give them true happiness.

7

THE MORAL SITUATION

The increasingly immoral conduct of today's society reflects the thinking of twentieth-century teachers, authors, artists, and playwrights. On every hand, accepted moral standards are being attacked as a product of outmoded religious ideas, or ignored by thoughtless people living to gratify their lusts. Biblical statements forbidding theft, murder, fornication, adultery, falsehood, and blasphemy are not esteemed worthy of serious consideration. Many insist that society needs a new moral code to replace the discarded standards. This moral system may come from men who profess no religious faith whatsoever, or it may be the product of so-called Christian leaders who deny faith in a personal God as revealed in the Bible. Consequently, mankind in general is accepting guidelines for conduct which originate either from those who make no pretension of being religious, or those who claim to be Christian but deny the basic doctrines of historic Christianity.

I. ELEMENTS OF NATURALISTIC MORALITY

Man cannot avoid making some determinations regarding right and wrong. Even those who accept the teaching of naturalistic evolution, and look upon man as essentially an animal, admit that some guidelines must be established. They may disagree in defining what is right and wrong in particular cases, and may have different norms by which they judge the moral quality of an act, but all of them agree that no fixed standard of conduct exists. They are unanimous in affirming that the Biblical or Christian approach to moral living is antiquated and inadequate. We will consider three important features in the thinking of present-day naturalistic moralists – determinism, hedonism, and utilitarianism.

The deterministic theory denies the reality of guilt. Modern secular morality teaches that men are not truly free and responsible personalities who stand condemned in the presence of a holy God. In fact, the term "guilty" is quite out of date, for two reasons. First, the majority of educators insist that no God exists who holds man responsible for his iniquities. Secondly, they consider man to be an animal; therefore, human intelligence is looked upon as a result of a process much like that which feeds information into a computer. A person who commits a terrible crime against society is said to be merely the victim of unfortunate programming.

This idea that man's nature has been predetermined by heredity and psychological factors has been strengthened by the teaching of Sigmund Freud. He theorized that all are victims of repressed unconscious complexes, such as the sex drives, called "libido." He portrayed man as a machine, programmed in his "unconscious" to react with conditioned responses. Therefore a person can never he held responsible for what he does.

This negation of guilt has contributed to a lenient attitude toward the criminal. He is treated as one who is ill, not punished as one who is evil. Significantly, however, the disastrous results of this thinking have been noted by a large percentage of psychiatrists and criminologists. Many of them today are emphasizing anew that man is a responsible creature, and that he must have a set of moral values by which he can regulate his life. They contend that practical considerations alone make it mandatory that both children and adults be held accountable for their conduct. The idea that man is a mere animal, meaning that all his actions are only responses to psychological stimuli, has been proven both dangerous and false. It has been abandoned by many former adherents.

Although a large percentage who have returned to a belief in man's freedom and responsibility are not Christians, they are moving closer to the Biblical doctrine of man. The Bible teaches that man was created in the image of God, and that he possesses a mind with which he can reason, a will through which he can make decisions, and an emotional nature which enables him to love and hate, weep and rejoice. It recognizes man's deep feelings of sinfulness, and provides a remedy. The Bible does not deny man's guilt, but reveals the redeeming grace of God through Jesus Christ. It tells people that they may be forgiven. The Scriptures also speak of inner conflict, and tell us how to achieve victory in the struggle to overcome indwelling sin. They declare that God implants a new life in those who turn to Him, and that the Holy Spirit takes up His residence in the body of every Christian. The Biblical concept of man is humiliating but ennobling, realistic, yet gloriously hopeful. A person who believes what the Bible says can be happy. This stands in sharp contrast to the wretchedness of the person who tries to face life's problems with the idea that he is "nothing."

The second characteristic of modern secular morality is its emphasis upon pleasure as the proper goal of life. This is a revival of the ancient philosophy called hedonism which contends that man is not to suppress certain instincts because of fear that he will violate God's law. It holds that the only real criterion by which man can make a decision regarding moral conduct is a determination of what will bring the greatest amount of genuine enjoyment. One may have to choose between momentary gaiety or that which will be ultimately more pleasurable, but basically every decision is selfish.

The hedonistic attitude toward life is both inadequate and destructive. Man is an individual, but he is also a social creature. He lives as part of a family and a community. A society cannot truly flourish if people are always thinking in terms of "me" instead of "we." When the Greek civilization adopted the hedonistic philosophy of life, it gradually corrupted from within, tottered and fell. The Roman civilization which followed was, for a time, made up of well-disciplined people, trained soldiers, generally honest political leaders, and impartial judges. However, its leaders accepted hedonism, and the Roman Empire soon became immoral, soft, and lethargic. The fiber of the once self-disciplined people deteriorated so that the Goths were able to swarm over the walls of Rome and destroy the civilization that could have provided such a favorable climate for the Christian faith.

Our own day parallels remarkably the Roman civilization. Democracy provides an atmosphere in which the Christian faith ought to flourish, in which liberty and justice should be extended to all men, and the material benefits of a rich land be shared by all its citizens. America has the potential to be a great force for God and righteousness, but a selfish pleasure-oriented philosophy of life has marred much of her history. If our nation continues to make a god out of pleasure, we will go the way of Greece and Rome. Ironically, whenever people make selfish enjoyment their goal, they fail to find happiness.

Many non-Christian moralists reject hedonism, however, and have substituted a philosophy called utilitarianism. They recognize that hedonism is too selfish and that it brings with it disastrous social consequences. Utilitarianism is a more noble approach to morality, substituting the principle of the greatest good for the greatest number in place of the idea that the agent's own happiness is the goal and standard of moral living. Furthermore, it looks upon certain pleasures as having greater intrinsic value than others, and gives them a higher degree of moral authority.

Utilitarianism fails because it does not provide objective norms. The individual is left to define for himself what will bring about the greatest good for the greatest number. One person might conceivably conclude that every physically deformed or mentally handicapped person should be put to death. Another might decide that the annihilation of a specific racial or religious group would be for the greatest good of the greatest number. A son could conclude that the death of his abusive father would be for the benefit of his mother and the members of the family. Utilitarianism does not really establish meaningful guidelines for erring sinners, and therefore has failed. A society which follows this system of thought will never achieve true happiness in the midst of a changing world.

II. THE NEW MORALITY OF MODERN THEOLOGY

A few decades ago a minister of the Gospel could be counted upon to speak in favor of legislation outlawing pornographic literature, obscene pictures, and dirty movies. Today, however, clergymen often lead in the battle for greater permissiveness in the area of morals. They are among the first to denounce the man who says that the Bible contains laws, rules, and moral principles which are to regulate conduct. They call this a "puritanical approach," giving the impression that those great people who eked out a living from the rocky soil, built our earliest colleges, and originated our literature, were a sick, neurotic, and guilt-ridden society. Today's religious leaders overlook the many excellent qualities of the Puritans, concentrating upon their preoccupation with sin and guilt, their severity, and their melancholy sternness. In this attitude, a number of modern clergymen have devised moral guidelines without accepting Biblical rules and regulations as absolutely authoritative. This system has sometimes been called "the new morality" and at other times is referred to as "situation ethics."

The two leading exponents of the new morality, Bishop John A. T. Robinson and Professor Joseph Fletcher, emphasize that moral conduct is not to be determined by laws, rules, or principles, but only by love as applied in the particular situation. In a series of six propositions, Dr. Fletcher sets forth his "theology of ethics." He declares: (1) the only thing intrinsically good is love; (2) when a Christian must make a decision regarding conduct he is not to think of moral laws or precepts, but is to make his decision on the basis of love; (3) love and justice are really the same thing, for justice is love distributed; (4) true love will desire good even for our enemies; (5) the end justifies the means when the aim is the expression of love; and (6) all of our decisions regarding moral conduct are to be made on the basis of love as applied to a particular situation.

The new morality exponents say that we must not look to the Bible for absolute principles, laws, or rules. Dr. Robinson states, "For nothing can of itself always be labeled as 'wrong.' One cannot, for instance, start from the position that 'sex relations before marriage' or 'divorce' are wrong or sinful in themselves. They may be in 99 cases or even 100 cases out of 100, but they are not intrinsically so, for the only intrinsic evil is the lack of love." * He goes on in this same book to point out that a young man should decide about his relations with a girl by asking, "How much do I love her?", not by considering the degree of sinfulness involved.

The same approach is advocated in relation to every aspect of moral conduct. If a person in a special situation believes that stealing would be consistent with love, he

* *Honest to God* (Philadelphia, 1963), p. 118.

may steal without feeling that he is breaking a law of God. The individual, according to the "new morality" theologians, must only be certain that it was actually "the love principle" that led him to steal for someone with a real need. These modern theologians contend that one is not to decide in advance whether or not he would steal if given the opportunity. Only when the situation presents itself can the decision be made.

The new morality is not Biblical, and does not deserve to be termed "Christian." It cannot be accepted by anyone who believes in the holy, living, personal God of our Christian faith. It misinterprets the Biblical relationship between law and love, and is open to criticism for being incomplete and inadequate on at least two counts. In the first place, it possesses a deficient view of man as a sinner. Secondly, it fails to provide for human weakness.

Those who advocate the new morality take for granted that all men will know what love means, and that they will correctly apply the love principle in every situation. This way of thinking overlooks man's depravity. It is possible for people to use the word "love" and still justify in their own minds acts of violence and cruelty. Recently, a student at a large university killed a co-ed because he felt he "loved her so much." Sinful man can twist the word "love" to have many meanings providing an excuse for almost every kind of evil deed.

The new morality also fails to provide for human weakness. To say that moral conduct is never to be determined in advance by reference to a standard or law, but situationally at the moment the decision must be made, is to place too much responsibility upon sin-weakened humans. In a moment of passion, one could easily act against better judgment. Two young people alone will be far more apt to behave properly if they determine in advance that since God demands purity, they will abstain from sexual sin. In an intimate situation, they are not going to think through the so-called "love principle." They need to be fortified by an advance decision that they will obey God's laws.

Some have the mistaken idea that people do better without definite guidelines. However, just the opposite is being proved. If a child is not given specific standards, he often rebels. He may act in a very irresponsible manner, but he is wondering all the while if anyone will care enough to stop him. Adults also possess a deep realization that they need guidelines, and they will keep trying from within to create principles by which they can live. Man in his human weakness needs specific laws for conduct, and many contemporary thinkers are beginning to realize this fact. The only way one can find happiness in this changing world is through faith in the God who is revealed in the holy Scriptures. A Christian knows what God wants him to do and has found forgiveness when he is conscious that he has failed.

8

SECULAR PHILOSOPHY OF SEX

In modern society the subject of sex is freely and frankly discussed on every hand. Its commercialization has become accepted as part of our way of life. Advertisements feature scantily dressed women and brazenly suggestive slogans and songs. Many children grow up in homes broken by divorce or stained by marital infidelity. A disheartening percentage of high school and college age youth are promiscuous in sexual conduct. Conditions are deteriorating so rapidly that Dr. Reinhold Niebuhr, by no means an evangelical Christian, expressed alarm in connection with the Kinsey Report saying that we are "approaching the license which characterized the Roman civilization in the period of its decay."

A number of factors have contributed to this situation. The idea that man is an animal, and the teaching that standards of the Christian faith have no divine authority, have eliminated the concept of sin and guilt before God. Society in general has become very open-minded, so that social stigma no longer exerts a strong restraining influence. Inexpensive and easily obtained preventives for pregnancy have removed another deterrent to extra-marital relationships. Furthermore, World War II and subsequent conflicts called for the mobilization of large numbers of young men, removing them from the restraining influence of their homes. Concentrated in areas where liquor and sex were dangled before them by those who were interested only in making money, it was easy for such young men to reason that they should enjoy themselves in view of the uncertainty of their future. Another contributing factor has been the industrial situation which is taking a large percentage of women out of their homes and putting them in the offices and factories where they work side by side with men. The automobile and motel have played a part by making illicit excursions easy and convenient.

Bible-believing Christians cannot be complacent in the face of this moral breakdown. They must stand up against this kind of immorality, for our civilization is doomed unless these grievous sins against God are checked. They acknowledge that some Christians in past generations did not always have a proper viewpoint of sex, but they also insist that present-day attitudes and standards are in error and destructive.

At least four distinct attitudes toward sex are being expressed in our society. This chapter will consider these false views so that we can better present the truth. It will also summarize the Biblical principles regarding sex, and will show that true happiness can be found only when one walks in obedience to God's moral law.

I. A Tainted Necessity

Many religious people have considered sex something distasteful, a subject not to be discussed more than is absolutely necessary. Parents did all they could to hide the facts of life from their children. When a baby was expected in the home no one spoke openly about it because pregnancy caused some degree of embarrassment.

This attitude toward sex as something shameful began early in the history of the Christian church, not with the Puritans as is often supposed. Some believers were influenced by Greek thought, which exalted the spiritual nature of man but had a very low concept of his physical being. The body was concluded to be sensual and sinful, and true virtue consisted in denying its natural desires, neglecting it, or abusing it. Marriage began to be looked upon as far less desirable than celibacy. However, upon a misinterpretation of Paul's words that "It is better to marry than to burn" (1 Corinthians 7:9), these early Christians sanctioned marriage. They even made it a sacrament because they saw its purpose as the founding of families for state and church. The sexual relationship was thus "justified" by marriage, only because it was the means by which the human race is procreated. It was not thought of as an expression of love, and its only recognized purpose was the begetting of children. For this reason the subject was not discussed, the facts of life were withheld from children, and pregnancy was a reluctant admission that something a bit shameful had taken place.

This concept of sex and the marriage relationship is not Biblical. It completely overlooks the wonderful truths relating to marriage and its purpose as set forth in the Scriptures. This distorted view of sex originated in the pagan world, and was introduced into Christendom through the influence of Grecian religion and philosophy.

II. The Ultimate Experience

The second false theory of sex makes it the ultimate experience of life. In fact, some contemporary authors of pornographic literature have practically deified it. They write on the premise that man is but the product of blind chance, nothing more than a physical organism. This rationalistic concept assigns to man no real identity, no worth, and no significance. It holds that the male can acquire a certain amount of authenticity through sex, and can at least attain the illusion that he is somebody. As the aggressor he gains the sense of achievement, and gives himself the false impression of power. The woman is said to have an instinctive need to belong to someone. She is presented as gladly yielding to a man, even when it means beatings and pain, in order to be possessed by someone or something. Yes, a number of today's pornographic writers and artists have a vague hope that, through free sexual expression, they will achieve a "religious experience." The tragedy is, however, that the unrestrained exercise of sexuality produces only an illusion of power and belonging. Like the use of drugs or psychedelic music it can never satisfy the deepest needs of the human heart. It never leads to genuine happiness or satisfaction.

III. A Mere Biological Function

The most popular of all current concepts maintains that sexual activity is a mere physical function which should be satisfied. Sex is looked upon as a physical need like eating and drinking, and is something which man has in common with the animals. The popular paperbacks and magazines which either consciously or unconsciously set forth this philosophy insist that it is harmful for people to suppress the sexual instinct. They teach that whenever two people mutually agree they should have no compunctions about sexual activity outside of marriage. They hold that divorce should be by mutual consent, and that we must cast off the so-called "puritanical" teachings of the Christian faith.

The results of this permissiveness have been tragic. The idea that sexual relationship in humans is nothing more than a biological function to be fulfilled without regard for morals is producing thousands upon thousands of destroyed lives. Mental and emotional disorders among college students are making necessary the services of more and more psychologists and psychiatrists. Institutions treating mental disorders are sadly overcrowded. Dr. Francis Braceland, former President of the American Psychiatric Association and currently editor of the *American Journal of Psychiatry* said, "A more lenient attitude about pre-marital sex experience has imposed stresses upon some women severe enough to cause emotional breakdown." In addition, our country now is plagued by some 200,000 cases of venereal disease per year, and illegal abortions are estimated to take place nearly a million times annually. Adding to these facts the tragic results of broken homes, it becomes obvious that our nation will not long remain great and strong unless this concept of the sexual function is abolished.

The writers of pornographic magazines and paperbacks make every effort to prove that religious parents who demand high moral standards produce sexual criminals and deviates. Not one shred of evidence substantiates this charge. (In fact, hardly any known sexual criminals come from Bible-believing homes.) The term "puritanical" is used improperly to describe a tyrannical parent, though he may have no religious inclinations whatsoever. Acts of sexual violence and perversion are the product of a society where a permissive attitude is practiced.

Another valid criticism of the permissive attitude is its basic selfishness. Each person thinks only in terms of his own pleasure or fulfillment. The basis of this approach is hedonism, a moral philosophy proven to be inadequate and dangerous. An individual cannnot be thinking only in terms of himself if he is to be a good member of society. Then, too, this attitude is completely slanted to serve the interest of the young male. It encourages him to make as many conquests as he can, both for the fulfillment of his sexual drive and for the bolstering of his own ego. A girl is expected to be a ready accomplice willing to give herself to one who does not necessarily love her, and may never want her as his own. It glamorizes sexual freedom for young attractive people, but provides nothing for those past middle age, or who are not physically appealing. Human beings need love and the feeling that they are needed and wanted, and mere biological sexual activity does not provide these basic human requirements. Many who have followed this kind of illicit love-making are today in a state of bitter disillusionment and agonizing despair.

IV. New Morality's "Love Principle"

A number of present-day theologians recognize that man is not a mere animal, and that love is a most vital ingredient in the marriage relationship. However, they are unwilling to accept the authoritative regulations of the Bible, and have included a system of sexual ethics in their "new morality." It is the application of situational ethics to sexual conduct. These theologians teach that one must not decide on the basis of rules or regulations what to do in a given situation. The determining factor is the "love principle," the seeking of the good of one's neighbor.

The motive presented in this approach to sexual conduct is better than the idea that the sexual relationship is nothing more than a biological phenomenon. However, it makes an impossible demand upon young people, asking them to think through the logical implications of the "love principle" when they are under the pressure of natural desire. A writer declares that this is "quite a long thought for an eighteen-year-old during the passionate moment in the back seat of a car." The word "love" is ambiguous. Young people may think they are in love, when in reality they have not yet discovered its true meaning. A married man may convince himself that he is in love with another woman, thus excusing immoral conduct as he perpetrates an act of base cruelty toward his wife. Young people need to have a high concept of life's sacredness and must decide in advance that they will maintain sexual purity. Under the stress that sometimes enters family life, a husband and wife must work out their problems to preserve their marriage, believing it is sacred, and that it is a lifelong and exclusive agreement. Absolute moral imperatives cannot be set aside with impunity. Broken homes, blighted lives, and perverted relationships always follow violation of God's moral laws.

The Bible teaches us that the sexual association of marriage is one of God's good provisions for mankind. Its purpose is the procreation of the human race and the tender expression of deep and abiding love. Marriage is an exclusive "one flesh" union, and that sexual expression of love within wedlock has deep significance. However, man has become a sinner, and often abuses or perverts all of God's good gifts, including sex. Therefore the Bible strongly condemns pre-marital relationships, unfaithfulness and homosexual conduct. Both the sanctity of marriage and a warning against all forms of impurity are clearly expressed in Hebrews 13:4.

> Marriage is honorable in all, and the bed undefiled,
> but fornicators and adulterers God will judge.

God's favor and blessing cannot rest upon the individual or nation which flouts His revealed will. Real satisfaction and joy can be found only when we walk the pathway of obedience to the Scriptures.

9

BIBLICAL THEOLOGY OF SEX

The Christian faith provides salvation from sin's penalty and power and its truths involve the whole man, body and soul, for time and eternity. The Bible presents a total world and life view, including principles for sexual conduct in our turbulent age. It teaches that sexuality is one of God's good provisions for mankind, not linking these desires or capacities to either the fall or the animal world. God created Adam and Eve as male and female, and it was before they fell into sin that He issued to them the command, "Be fruitful, and multiply, and fill the earth . . ." (Genesis 1:28). Even if sin had not entered the human race, the means of procreation would have been through sexual union. Therefore, a Bible-believing Christian will not approach the study of sexuality with the attitude that the subject is somewhat sinful or shameful by its very nature. He will recognize it to be ordained by God, and important to his individual life.

I. THE SIGNIFICANCE OF MARRIAGE

The marriage relationship is of deep significance in the mind of God. While it includes physical sexual union as an important ingredient, marriage is far more than a mere conjunction of bodies. God has graciously provided it for the completion and expression of the human personality.

The creation story indicates that God first made Adam a solitary male in the midst of a world where animals lived in pairs. The Lord assigned him the task of naming the animals in the garden of Eden, and Adam became aware of the fact that every male had a mate except him, and that no form of animal life was suited to his need. He realized his incompleteness as a solitary individual, and was prepared for the gift of a female counterpart to be at his side. The Bible depicts the beautiful scene as God created Eve to be Adam's companion.

> And the Lord God caused a deep sleep to fall upon Adam, and he slept: and he took one of his ribs, and closed up the flesh instead thereof;
> And the rib, which the Lord God had taken from man, made he a woman, and brought her unto the man (Genesis 2:21, 22).

Since the woman was made from the man, she is dependent upon him, and is not complete without him. Similarly, the man is incomplete without her. They need each other, and only within wedlock can this full requirement be met. The Genesis account, after describing Adam's reaction to the lovely woman taken from his side, declares,

> Therefore shall a man leave his father and his mother, and shall cleave unto his wife; and they shall be one flesh (Genesis 2:24).

The word "cleave" means "to glue oneself to something." The man, who is stronger, is responsible to cling to his wife. He finds fulfillment of his personality in possessing, while the wife will fulfill her role being possessed by her husband's strong and enduring love.

Not only do the two sexes require one another for the completion of their own personalities, they also need each other for the full expression of themselves in their mental, emotional, and volitional powers. Sexual union within wedlock involves a communication of the self to another. The sex act is never to be considered a mere physical and meaningless deed. Therefore, the Biblical term "to know," used to designate the sexual act, is more than a delicacy of expression. This same word is used to indicate knowledge of God in many Scripture passages (Judges 2:10; Jeremiah 22:16), and states that in the mutual self-giving of the sexual relationship within wedlock exists a communication of total being. Self-awareness and self-identity are heightened through the sexual aspect of marriage. Manhood and womanhood are most deeply communicated in this tender expression of love.

The Bible clearly renounces all promiscuity. The conjugal act is rich in significance, and therefore can be exercised only within wedlock. The sexual relationship is never a merely casual act. The most popular concept of sex today holds that it is merely a biological function with no meaning, but this is completely contrary to the principles of the Word of God. The apostle Paul states that illicit relationships, commercial and offhand as they may be, are matters of profound import, for they involve the total personality. Any extra-marital act, even with a prostitute, scars the deep hidden bond of marriage. Therefore Paul says,

> What? Know ye not that he who is joined to an harlot is one body? For two, saith he, shall be one flesh (1 Corinthians 6:16).

Since the relationship of wedlock is so important, the Word of God contains literally scores of warnings against incest, adultery, and fornication. The Bible also condemns in unequivocal terms all homosexuality, and every other form of perversion. God gave instructions to Israel in Leviticus 18 relating to their sexual conduct, and, after explicitly condemning the sins of homosexuality and bestiality, declared,

> Defile not ye yourselves in any of these things; for in all these the nations are defiled, which I cast out before you.
> And the land is defiled; therefore I do visit the iniquity thereof upon it, and the land itself vomiteth out her inhabitants (Leviticus 18:24, 25).

The gift of sex, which God intended for the expression of deep, rich, and tender love, as well as the procreation of the human race, is twisted into something ugly and shameful through these perversions. They do not contribute to one's self-awareness or self-identity in manhood or womanhood. In fact, these practices are destructive, and are condemned by the apostle Paul in Romans 1 as the culmination of the disastrous consequences of unbelief.

Though the sexual deviate in some cases may be mentally ill and in need of treatment instead of punishment, the Christian is never in any way to give help to those who are minimizing its intrinsic evil or its potential harm. One of the great tragedies of our age is the increasing incidence and influence of homosexuality. Organizations are seeking to make it an accepted way of life. In books and periodicals, on radio and television it is joked about in a light-hearted vein. Some have estimated that at least twenty-five percent of the people working in the American entertainment world are confirmed homosexuals. If this is true, our nation is ripe for God's judgment.

II. THE EXCLUSIVENESS OF MARRIAGE

The second chapter of Genesis lays the foundation for the Biblical truth that marriage was established by God to be a relationship between *two* people, a man and his wife. Though polygamy was practiced in the Old Testament days, even by some godly men, it was never sanctioned by God. Genesis 2:24 declares, "Therefore shall a man leave his father and his mother, and shall cleave unto his wife; and they shall be one flesh."

The term "one flesh" speaks of far more than physical union. It sets forth marriage as bringing about the adjoining of two personalities. The Lord Jesus quoted these words from Genesis when the Pharisees asked Him concerning His teaching on divorce. He explicitly declared that marriage is a divinely wrought fusion of two people, and that men have no right to capriciously dissolve this union.

> And he answered and said unto them, Have ye not read that he who made them at the beginning, made them male and female;
> And said, For this cause shall a man leave father and mother, and shall cleave to his wife, and they two shall be one flesh?
> Wherefore, they are no more two, but one flesh. What, therefore, God hath joined together, let no man put asunder (Matthew 19:4-6).

The Lord Jesus further stated that the only basis upon which a marriage may be ended is fornication. The person who becomes unfaithful, engaging in sexual relations with another, violates the "one flesh" unity which is the very heart of marriage. The essence of the oneness of husband and wife is blemished when one member engages in extra-marital sexual activity.

This sacred exclusiveness of the "one flesh" tie is also emphasized by the apostle Paul.

> For this cause shall a man leave his father and mother, and shall be joined unto his wife, and they two shall be one flesh.

> This is a great mystery, but I speak concerning Christ
> and the church (Ephesians 5:31, 32).

Through sexual union, the husband and wife are brought into a vital relationship with one another. Marriage expresses love so deep, so self-sacrificing, so tender and pure that it is likened to the union that exists between Christ and His Church. These verses declare that the redeeming love of God through Christ is beyond understanding. Men cannot comprehend the love which prompted the Father to give His Son into the dreaded darkness and anguish of Calvary, nor the marvel that through union with Christ God will someday receive them in glory as His peculiar possession. This marvelous love, this inexpressibly glorious unity of Christ and His people, is reflected here on earth in the marriage relationship. A more noble description of the oneness of husband and wife has never been presented. A higher concept is impossible to imagine.

This majestic view of marriage places upon every husband the solemn responsibility to reveal in his love for his wife the marks of Christ's love for His Church. The husband is to show her self-sacrificing and unchanging devotion. The wife is to respect and honor the one who reaches out in devotion to her. Thus both express their love for God by obeying the injunction of His Word,

> Nevertheless, let every one of you in particular so love
> his wife even as himself; and the wife, see that she rev-
> erence her husband (Ephesians 5:33).

III. THE PRACTICAL IMPLICATIONS OF MARRIAGE

The "one flesh" nature of marriage, with the intimacy and sacredness it implies, is a powerful plea for chastity, both before and after the wedding ceremony. Adultery and promiscuity are implicitly condemned, and polygamy is eliminated. A person cannot relate physically, emotionally, intellectually, and spiritually in the marriage relationship to more than one person.

Marriage indeed is honorable, and the sexual relationship within wedlock is deeply significant. It must never be considered shameful or tainted, nor should it be looked upon as given solely for the purpose of human procreation. It is a deep, rich, and meaningful expression of tender love. Therefore, the writer of Hebrews declares,

Marriage is honorable in all, and the bed undefiled, but fornicators and adulterers God will judge (Hebrews 13:4).

A Christian couple should be conscious of these Biblical truths regarding their sexuality. They must look upon the conjugal relationship as an important aspect of their marriage, and should never think of it in terms of animal passion. The husband, whose love is marked by self-sacrifice, patience, and understanding, will usually find his wife to be submissive, responsive, and loving. Children in such a home receive immeasurable benefit from the spirit of harmony and love which prevails. They will more easily obey the Scriptural injunction,

Children, obey your parents in the Lord; for this is right.

Honor thy father and mother (which is the first commandment with promise),

That it may be well with thee, and thou mayest live long on the earth (Ephesians 6:1-3).

10

BIBLICAL THEOLOGY OF ETHICS

Modern man by accepting the theory of naturalistic evolution looks upon human life as essentially no different from the animal world. Such thinking denies man's moral responsibility and sharply defines the futility of human life. The person who tries to think through issues and longs to find some meaning in life can only cry out in despair as long as he accepts this godless system of thought. As a result, many have turned to drugs, sexual orgies, psychedelic music, pornographic literature and art in an attempt to escape the logical implications of their denial of God.

The only answer to the dilemma of twentieth-century man is the historic Christian faith, taught in the New Testament and preached by the apostles. That faith still lives in churches where the great historic doctrines are believed, and where the Bible is acknowledged as the Word of God. Reaffirming our confidence in the absolute standards of Biblical Christianity, let us consider the fact of the existence of God and moral law; secondly, the relation of law and human freedom; thirdly, the connection between law and love; and fourthly, the application of these principles in our sin-tainted world.

I. THE EXISTENCE OF GOD AND MORAL LAW

The Bible does not present a series of logical arguments to prove God's existence. It begins with the simple affirmation, "In the beginning God. . . ."

Belief or unbelief in relation to God is basically a moral problem. The issue is not settled on the basis of logic alone. This does not mean, however, that a Christian cannot give good reasons for his faith. He can remind unbelievers that life, even that of the simplest cell, is so complex and highly complicated that it points to an intelligent designer and creator. He can also point to himself as a thinking, emotional, and volitional personality, and ask how blind chance could have produced such a being. In fact, man's characteristics are so distinctive when compared to the animal that even thorough-going evolutionists admit that "there is a fundamental difference between the mind of man and nonman. This difference is one of kind, not one of degree." * The unbeliever must exercise more faith to hold his evolutionary theory than the Christian does to believe in God. And when the atheist or agnostic says that man is not a genuine personality, he is setting himself against the testimony of human experience. Sensitive people cannot live with the concept that man is merely a programmed machine. Therefore, in spite of all the efforts of brilliant men to answer the problems of man's origin and nature, they remain a mystery unless one believes what the Bible says.

The person and work of Jesus Christ are also valid evidences for the existence of God and the truth of the Bible. The Old Testament depicts the course of history and prophecy leading up to Christ's actual coming to earth, and the gospels present a record of His life, His words, and His great redemptive work. The significance of His substitutionary death, burial, and resurrection is explained in the epistles, and the message of the New Testament has exercised a transforming power in the lives of those who have believed it.

Belief in God as He is revealed in the Bible has certain logical implications. A holy God cannot be indifferent to moral conduct. Therefore, a moral law exists as the expression of that holiness of which John spoke when he declared, "God is light" (1 John 1:5). The Lord is completely free from all impurity and defilement, and therefore cannot approve of evil. God's very nature demands that He make a distinction between right and wrong. Man, by virtue of his original creation in God's image, possesses, even in his fallen state, an innate consciousness of good and evil. This implies the existence of a moral law behind all the written expressions of God's holy will. Murder, theft, adultery, dishonesty, and the like violate God's nature. Kindness,

* Leslie A. White, *The Symbol: The Origin and Basis of Human Behavior,* p. 230.

purity, honesty, and truthfulness are in harmony with His holy nature. God's principles of right and wrong underlie the Mosaic legislation as well as the explicit commands in the New Testament. Although these very principles are denied by many present-day theologians, yet it remains true that every system of ethics not reckoned with God and His holiness is Biblically wrong and historically has been proven inadequate. Sin must be seen in its relationship to God, and must be recognized as a violation of His will.

You may deny God, live immorally, and ridicule the idea of an unchanging moral law if you will. You may even think you are doing so because you are too intelligent to believe the message of the Bible. However, your unbelief cannot be based upon your reason, because you have left many questions unanswered. Your denial of God stems from your sinful nature. In your pride of intellect you have rejected God, and the Bible warns that you will suffer the consequences in a life of ever-increasing enslavement and hopelessness. In Romans 1 Paul declares:

> Professing themselves to be wise, they became fools,
>   And even as they did not like to retain God in their knowledge, God gave them over to a reprobate mind, to do those things which are not seemly (Romans 1: 22, 28).

II. GOD'S MORAL LAW AND FREEDOM

Many current thinkers in the realm of personal ethics use the term "freedom" in a paradoxical manner. On the one hand, they view a person as having ability only to act according to his individual nature; that is, in a predetermined manner depending upon certain psychological or environmental factors. On the other hand, these same moralists defend man's right to engage in pornography, sexual perversions, and other like practices by appealing to "freedom," the very quality they declare he does not possess. In so doing they are guilty of two errors: (1) they deny that man is able to make moral choices, and (2) they confuse liberty with license.

The created world confirms the Biblical teaching that true freedom is always expressed within certain boundaries or limits. The designer of an airplane has freedom, but he must work within the limitations of certain aerodynamic

77

principles to produce a plane both beautiful and efficient. Architects and scientists, working within natural laws, are able to construct buildings and mechanical devices of symmetry and beauty. Why? Because God has made an orderly universe. On the contrary, some modern artists and composers, who have despaired of finding significance in life, originate art and music in which the chaos of shape and sound expresses the hollowness of their empty philosophies.

In the spiritual realm, as in the material, man must choose to live within the framework of God's moral law. In so doing, he will practice the virtues of a beautiful life, and thereby glorify God and find personal fulfillment. The person who violates God's moral laws and from a false concept of freedom develops a life marked by cruelty, dishonesty, falsehood, and immorality is missing the purpose for which God made him. Biblical ethics recognizes that what a person becomes will be influenced to some extent by heredity or environmental factors, but insists that his deeds are determined from within, by choice, not by compulsion. It sets forth man as a free and responsible being.

If you, the reader, have thrown away all restraints, and are living to gratify the flesh, you are merely existing. You have chosen the wrong path, and because of that choice, you are personally responsible for what you do. The Bible teaches that continuance in this way will bring you endless woe. However, Jesus Christ offers you the eternal and abundant life. He declared that He came to enrich men, and give purpose and goal to life, when He said, ". . . I am come that they might have life, and that they might have it more abundantly" (John 10:10).

This "abundant life," characterized by real usefulness and significance, awaits all those who submit to the claims of Christ. The way to God and true satisfaction is through faith in the Lord Jesus. Life which is both everlasting and abounding is available.

IV. GOD'S MORAL LAW AND THE SITUATION

Non-biblical moralists have the mistaken idea that love cannot function under the restrictions of law, and claim that the application of the "love principle" is the true guide for living. Love and law are compatible, however, for no man can practice love without law, and no man can fulfill the demands of God's moral law without love. Obedience to specific laws is not necessarily legalism. The redeemed person who loves God and his fellow man does not grudgingly submit to God's laws, nor does he do so to gain merit points. Love enables a person to fulfill the divine demands, and then to go beyond the requirements of law.

The Lord Jesus declared that the essence of law is love. In summarizing the ten comandments, He said that they are fulfilled when one loves God supremely and one's neighbor as oneself (see Matthew 22:37-40).

The apostle Paul as well affirmed the priority of love, and, like the Lord Jesus, did not deny the validity of God's specific commands. In fact, he listed five prohibitions found in the decalogue, stating that obedience to them could be obtained only through love (see Romans 13:9, 10).

Therefore, the Bible presents love as not simply a vague and general attempt to do that which is good for the other person, but carefully defines it by precepts, commandments, and moral imperatives. This eliminates the twisting of the "love principle" to justify murder, stealing, or other forms of immoral conduct. The believer, finding a life of obedience rich and rewarding, gratefully acknowledges the truth of 1 John 5:3, "For this is the love of God, that we keep his commandments: and his commandments are not burdensome."

IV. God's Moral Law and the Situation

The "new morality" theologians strongly emphasize that men sometimes must choose between two alternatives, neither of which is perfectly pure. They unjustly criticize Biblical morality, saying that it fails to consider such situations. They are wrong, for the Bible does relate many instances in which one moral principle was violated to preserve another, but it never vindicates the act. When a believer is placed in a situation where he is forced to do something that isn't right, he must accept the lesser of the evils, and then ask God to forgive him for the sin he could not avoid.

Let us suppose that a man in a country occupied by foreign enemy troops is approached by soldiers seeking his wife and daughters. Knowing that his loved ones may be sexually violated, he lies by telling the soldiers he does not know where they are. He sees the lie as less evil than the betraying of his family. An incident like this prompts the "new morality" teachers to hastily conclude that lying in itself is not wrong. We insist, however, that the lie the man told was sinful, and that it is always wrong to lie. The father sinned when he lied, and he should confess his sin to God. When he does, he may rejoice in the assurance that the Lord has indeed forgiven.

God's children positively assert that lying, stealing, immorality, and similar acts are evil under any and all circumstances. The believer's goal should be perfect conformity to the will of God. Nevertheless he must avoid a harsh legalism in regard to the sin of others. A fellow believer who has sinned is in need of Christian love and sympathy. We must emulate the Lord Jesus who showed compassion toward the woman caught in the act of adultery. He was considerate of her, rebuked her enemies, forgave her sin, and enjoined her from henceforth to live a pure life. By precept the apostle Paul confirmed what our Lord indicated by example when he said,

> Brethren, if a man be overtaken in a fault, ye who are spiritual restore such an one in the spirit of meekness, considering thyself, lest thou also be tempted (Galatians 6:1).

Bible-believing Christians therefore will manifest understanding and love, but will not make the mistake of the new moralists who sacrifice God's absolute standards of right and wrong. Christians will never call wrong things right or right things wrong, and will never justify evil. Even when the situation makes it necessary for him to choose the lesser of two evils, he acknowledges his sin to God when he makes his choice. God's standards are absolute. They cannot be annulled or modified.

The way to genuine happiness in this changing world is through a life of obedience to God's holy law. You can know God's will through the study of His Word. In addition, when you submit yourself to Jesus Christ, the Holy Spirit will enable you to live for God's glory and your neighbor's welfare. You will find true happiness in the midst of a changing world.

11

THE PROBLEM OF KNOWLEDGE

Young people of every age feel a certain amount of intellectual superiority over their parents. They more readily adjust to the new conditions of a constantly changing world, and balk at the caution exercised by older people. Furthermore, the young are always idealistic, and wonder why the previous generation has not made more progress toward the attainment of the better life. They have not learned by experience the problems that are encountered when pressing toward the achievement of lofty goals, nor do they properly appreciate the benefits they enjoy because of the efforts of their parents. Few young people see life and history in proper perspective, and therefore a generation gap has always existed.

Today, however, the gulf between youth and those who are over thirty has taken on a new dimension. Previous generations tended to cooperate with progressive adults, and this tempered their impatience. Many young people today exhibit the same attitude, but the activists who are rioting and demonstrating do not trust adults, possess little appreciation for the accomplishments of past generations, and have no true understanding of the complexity of life's problems. The activists declare that Moses, Plato, Aristotle, the apostle Paul, and even Jesus Christ, have said nothing worthy of serious consideration for today's world. Therefore they reject the past as a source of information, and refuse to look to God for help. These militant young people have a mistaken concept of knowledge, authority, freedom, and happiness.

This chapter will present an examination of the prevailing erroneous concept of knowledge which contends that faith in a personal God is an antequated concept disproven by science, and that man can solve his problems without appeal to the supernatural.

I. The Failure of Human Knowledge

All human knowledge which seeks to achieve its goals without God is doomed to failure. It has not been adequate to meet man's needs in the past, and has not solved his deepest problems today.

The ancients did not possess the technological skills of the machine age, but it would be a mistake to label them ignorant. More than 2000 years before Christ the Egyptians and Chaldeans constructed cities with great buildings, artistic sculpture, and active industry. Mathematics, law, and government were carefully studied and systematized, and great skill was developed in the arts of weaving, metal-working, and gem-engraving. Libraries, made up of clay tables on which letters were impressed, were collected even in this early day. Later, the classical Greek world could boast the great minds of Homer, Socrates, Plato, Aristotle, and others. The works of Homer and Plato still are studied in our colleges and universities, and Aristotle's principles of logic are yet to be surpassed. Yet none of these civilizations was able to endure. Each reached a zenith, deteriorated, and fell to hostile powers.

The bankruptcy of human knowledge is also demonstrated by the history of the Roman Empire. Its first citizens were efficient and disciplined, but barbaric, showing little regard for past civilization. The knowledge and arts of classical Greece, however, influenced the Romans, bringing about a culture known as the Greco-Roman civilization. But, sad to say, Greek culture, though containing some commendable features and producing great literature and philosophy, was pagan, degenerate, and corrupt. The Roman people lost the simplicity, frugality, and morality that had marked the earlier days, and became pleasure-mad, soft, and grossly immoral. The high intellectual perception of the great Greek philosophers slowly declined into inferior systems of thought and meaningless sophistries. Luke thus described the so-called intellects of his day:

> For all the Athenians and strangers who were there spent their time in nothing else, but either to tell, or to hear some new thing (Acts 17:21).

World conditions at the time of Christ and the early apostles were characterized by social unrest, moral disorder, and religious pessimism. The knowledge of Greece, even when coupled with the organizational genius of Rome, was unable to meet the needs of mankind. For this reason the apostle Paul glorified in the simplicity of the Gospel, declaring that it would accomplish that which human wisdom had failed to do. Man's wisdom does not lead to God. However, the good news of a crucified and risen Savior is God's power unto salvation.

> For the preaching of the cross is to them that perish foolishness; but unto us who are saved it is the power of God.
>
> For it is written, I will destroy the wisdom of the wise, and will bring to nothing the understanding of the prudent.
>
> Where is the wise? Where is the scribe? Where is the disputer of this age? Hath not God made foolish the wisdom of this world?
>
> For after that, in the wisdom of God, the world by wisdom knew not God, it pleased God by the foolishness of preaching to save them that believe.
>
> For the Jews require a sign, and the Greeks seek after wisdom;
>
> But we preach Christ crucified, unto the Jews a stumbling block, and unto the Gentiles foolishness;
>
> But unto them who are called, both Jews and Greeks, Christ the power of God, and the wisdom of God (1 Corinthians 1:18-24).

The cross was foolishness to the Greeks because it did not seem to have an intellectual basis. However, those who had believed the message and trusted Christ found in Him the power and wisdom of God. The Gospel is the power of God because it conquers sin, man's greatest enemy, and it is the wisdom of God because it shows that He knew the real nature of man's failure and provided for it. All the sagacity of the Greek philosophers and all the noble grandeur of Grecian literature, combined with the Roman ability to maintain law, order and peace, were insufficient. World conditions continued to deteriorate and human life became increasingly meaningless. The contrasting light of the Gospel, against this backdrop of gloom and pessimism, strikingly demonstrated the inadequacy of human wisdom.

Stepping across the centuries to our present era, the same ineffectiveness of human wisdom is once again apparent to all who have eyes to see. A popular weekly news magazine recently mentioned the paradox of knowledge in our day. It pointed out that ninety percent of all the scientists of all time are now alive, and that mankind is on the threshold of almost unbelievable technological advances, designed to increase the availability of information. Computer libraries and microfilm reference works will soon electronically dispense organized information on every subject into any home or school. Machines now compute mathematical problems in two seconds which would take a man thirty-eight years to calculate. Yet, in spite of all this "instant knowledge," more and more people despair of understanding themselves or the world in which they live. As men learn more they become increasingly aware of the complexity of the universe, and of the fact that the problems of life have no simple solution.

The present world scene is far from attractive. The swollen abdomens and spindly limbs of those dying from protein deficiency bear eloquent testimony to the failure of man's great knowledge to provide food for all. The slums of large cities continue to grow. Airplanes drop their death-dealing bombs, and young men are wounded and killed in warfare more savage and cruel than that of any period in history. Assassinations, student violence, riots, broken homes, and spiraling crime rates all point to the failure of man's wisdom. Even in the "slave world" of Communism, people are discovering the truth of the words: "Man shall not live by bread alone." All of the twentieth century technological skill is insufficient to solve life's most important problems. Never has there been more unhappiness than in our present generation.

II. The Limits of Human Knowledge

Human knowledge has definite limitations, whether in the fields of natural science or in abstract studies like philosophy and psychology. The majority of today's people have accepted certain theories without question, and have rejected Biblical Christianity without investigation.

The theory of naturalistic evolution is often looked upon

as a scientifically proven fact. Honest men, however, acknowledge that those who seek to account for life without believing in God proceed on many unfounded presuppositions.

A study of the fossils does not provide proof for evolution, and careful scrutiny of the various theories of how life originated shows them to be nothing more than educated guesses.

When the atheistic scientist turns to fossils for proof, he finds that the lowest layers, the Cambrian level, represent a great variety of highly complex animals. These creatures show no evidence of having developed from one another, and point to no common source. Evolutionists say that over one and one-half billion years were required in the intricate development of these specimens. However, not one shred of evidence can be found to support the idea that life was present on earth earlier than the time indicated by these fossils. Paleontology therefore suggests that life appeared suddenly, in wide diversity, and in great complexity.

Furthermore, nothing has ever been found to verify the theory that reptiles gradually developed into birds, or birds into mammals. Millions of fossils have been discovered and classified, so that one would expect clear illustrations of the gradual change of reptiles into birds. However, such examples have not yet been discovered. When evolutionists point out that these organic remains are formed only under certain special conditions, and that therefore it is reasonable to conclude that few if any of these transitional forms happen to be fossilized, they are begging the question. Paleontologists are not dependent upon a few hundred or even a few thousand fossils for information, but upon millions. In spite of the failure of these remains to verify the theory of evolution, atheistic scientists consider this field of study to be the strongest evidence for their theory. Julian Huxley, in his *Discourses Biological and Geological*, said, "Primary and direct evidence in favor of evolution can be furnished only by paleontology." However, another staunch exponent of evolution, A. Franklin Shull, frankly admits that the study of fossils does not prove the theory. After reviewing the fossil records he makes the following statement: "Biologists have *assumed* genetic continuity because the alternative explanations have seemed incredible or impossible." *

We therefore conclude that fossils do not prove the theory of evolution. They do indeed indicate that a great change has taken place, but no evidence can be set forth to show that a dog and horse, for example, have a common ancestor. The first horse *may* have been a small animal with four toes, but if he were, he possessed built-in genetic potential to develop into the horse as we know him today. The fossil remains show no evidence that he was ever anything but a horse. The evolutionist fills in the gaps between the various forms of life by faith in his theory because he feels it to be more logical than believing in God. The Christian, however, recognizes the possibility of God's activity. No young person should be deluded into the idea that belief in the God who has revealed Himself in the Bible indicates ignorance. Nor should he be duped into believing that the science of paleontology teaches amoeba to man evolution.

The various theories propounded to explain how life began are fanciful and unsupported by evidence. Some biochemists theorize that life began when geochemical atmospheric conditions on the earth were much different from today. They conjecture that in this environment organic compounds were formed out of the primordial ooze, and that large amounts of chemical energy were thus accumulated. They contend that perhaps an electrical charge brought about the formation of protein molecules large enough to bear life. This theory faces many problems, and is by no means universally held by experts in the field. Christians need not view with alarm these ideas or the accompanying attempts by modern scientists to create life. Men are only bringing together some of the "stuff" that makes up life, and are discovering a little more about how God created it. The simplest cell is so complex and complicated that man has not been able to define it clearly, much less duplicate it. The affirmation of Genesis 1:1, "In the beginning God created the heavens and the earth," is a far better explanation of origin than anything man has been able to advance.

In the realm of philosophy, the same failure of human knowledge to explain life and provide happiness is apparent.

* *Evolution* (New York, 1936), p. 65.

Those who deny that God exists outside the space-time world as its Creator and Sustainer may be termed either naturalists or rationalists. Such people must explain all of life, including man, without reference to an external cause. In such thinking, man can only be the product of blind force, plus time and chance. It follows that since he is the product of irrational causes, he has no right to boldly affirm himself to be a rational creature. Professor J. B. S. Holdane, in his book *Possible Worlds,* makes this observation: "If my mental processes are determined wholly by the motions of atoms in my brain, I have no reason to suppose that my beliefs are true . . . and hence I have no reason to suppose my brain to be composed of atoms." The naturalist, if he is consistent, cannot affirm that man possesses valid reasoning powers, genuine emotions, and a free will. He must look upon man as wholly under the control of chemical processes or psychological factors that are part of "impersonal Nature."

This attitude toward the world and man has led to the virtual abandonment of metaphysical thinking. Most secular philosophers agree that no answer can be found to the ultimate questions of being: Who am I? Why am I here? Where am I going? In continental Europe many intellectuals have turned to a philosophy called existentialism. They affirm that we must accept life as meaningless — even absurd — but that somehow, through a non-rational feeling or act, we must seek an experience by which we will be "authenticated." In English-speaking countries the systems called logical positivism and definitionalism have a wide following. They present a case for working only with that data which is available for scientific evaluation. The logical positivist, however, must proceed on the assumption that the things he observes have objective validity, and that he himself possesses a rational mind. But he has no right to do this if he is consistent with his basic premise that man is a product of blind chance.

Both the existentialism of the European continent and the defining philosophies of England and America fail to answer any questions about ultimate truth, and therefore are in no position to deny God or spiritual realities. They proceed on the blind assumption that no personal Creator and Sustainer of the world exists, but this is something they are unable to prove. Man in his own wisdom is utterly at a loss to explain either himself or the world in which he lives. Therefore, true happiness can be found only when one submits himself to God's revelation.

III. THE ALTERNATIVES TO HUMAN KNOWLEDGE

The Christian unhesitatingly acknowledges the failures and limitations of human knowledge, but nevertheless insists that men need not despair. He has found in Jesus Christ the answer to life's vexing problems. He knows who man is, why he is here, and where he is going. He does not credit himself with possessing a more penetrating intellect than the naturalist; rather, he declares that this knowledge and peace are available to all.

The Christian life begins with an act of faith. The historical Christ is revealed in the four gospels, and the significance of His life, death, and resurrection is explained in the epistles. The New Testament books have been thoroughly examined by critical scholarship, and their authenticity has been proved. We therefore have good reason to believe what they say about Jesus Christ. However, those who will not deviate from their naturalistic or rationalistic presuppositions refuse to believe, being influenced neither by historical evidence nor the testimony of the Christian Church. Therefore, they will not find joy or peace until they make a moral decision. They must acknowledge their bankruptcy and sinfulness, and in humble faith submit to the claims of Jesus Christ. When they do this, the Holy Spirit will make real the truths of the Scriptures, life will be filled with meaning, rich in joy, and glorious in expectation.

The words of the apostle Paul ring out to a generation plagued by restless uncertainties and despair:

> For the preaching of the cross is to them that perish foolishness; but unto us who are saved it is the power of God (1 Corinthians 1:18).

Malcolm Muggeridge, the brilliant satirist who once edited *Punch*, has observed the utter failure of humanistic thinking to meet the needs of mankind. He sees the world becoming increasingly lawless and immoral, and in his book *Another King* declares: "So I came back to where I began, to the other king, one Jesus, to the Christian notion that man's efforts to make himself personally and collectively happy

88

in earthly terms are doomed to failure. He must, indeed, as Christ said, be born again, be a new man, or he's nothing. So at least I have concluded, having failed to find in past experience, present dilemmas and future expectations, any alternative proposition." *

Yes, the crucified, risen, exalted and returning Christ is the only answer to man's deepest needs. Every restless soul should know that the power and wisdom of God is available to all who will believe the message of the Gospel.

* *Another King* (Edinburgh, 1968), pp. 12, 13.

12

THE PROBLEM OF AUTHORITY

The unhappiness and discontent of the present generation is strikingly displayed in the turbulent unrest of young people on the campuses of high schools, colleges, and universities. Many students insist they should have a stronger voice in the determination of school policy and curriculum requirements. The radical element shows little respect for teachers or administrative authorities, and as a result the general public is dismayed, some even demanding strong police action to subdue these revolutionaries. However, responsible adults recognize that though it may be necessary to expel some of these young people from our institutions of learning, this alone will not solve the basic problem. Campus revolt is but a symptom of a serious disease plaguing the whole world today, that of ungodliness. The rebellion against authority and the so-called "establishment" is not a sudden mysterious flareup, but the direct result of a gradual rejection of God's authority, which has taken place during the last fifty years. Therefore, many of the adults who so strongly express their dismay at the insurgence of these young people are themselves largely responsible. They have had a major part in producing today's disturbing conditions.

The Bible teaches that all authority is rooted in God. The opening chapters of Genesis present Him as the Creator of the universe, and as the Supreme Lawgiver to whom men must render obedience. From Genesis through Revelation the triune God is portrayed as the ultimate Authority, declaring His laws and indicating the consequences of disobedience. Woven throughout the fabric of the Old Testament is the recognition of God as King of the world — its Creator, Controller, Provider, and Savior. For example, the Psalms, the Hymnbook of the Hebrew faith, beautifully expresses this conviction:

> Oh, sing unto the Lord a new song; sing unto the Lord, all the earth.
> Say among the nations that the Lord reigneth. The world also shall be established that it shall not be moved; he shall judge the peoples righteously.
> Let the heavens rejoice, and let the earth be glad; let the sea roar, and the fullness thereof.
> Let the field be joyful, and all that is therein; then shall all the trees of the forest rejoice
> Before the Lord; for he cometh, for he cometh to judge the earth; he shall judge the world with righteousness, and the peoples with his truth (Psalm 96:1, 10-13).

In discussing the subject of authority, we will first consider the tragedy of its rejection both in theory and in practice, and secondly, the rationale for its acceptance today.

I. AUTHORITY — THE TRAGEDY OF ITS REJECTION

Everyone who observes and reads is aware of the great changes that have taken place in recent years with respect to moral conduct. People have always told lies, practiced dishonesty, acted cruelly, and committed immoral deeds, but most men and women were willing to admit that these things were wrong. They acknowledged that truthfulness, honesty, kindness and purity were desirable virtues. Today, however, many deny that a clear-cut distinction can be made between right and wrong, good and evil, and between guilt and innocence.

This present attitude which rejects absolute authority and definite standards has its origin in the theories of men in philosophy and science, and these ideas have gradually worked their way into the life pattern of the masses. The Bible clearly teaches that man is a rational creature with the responsibility to live in obedience to the moral laws of a personal God. Many early non-Christian philosophers, as well, generally having followed the rationalistic idealism of Plato or Aristotle, asserted that man is superior to other creatures, and that genuine distinctions of truth and morality are eternal and changeless. Even in relatively modern times, men like Descartes, Leibnitz, Hegel and Hocking considered man to be under obligation to obey fixed norms which he could not violate without painful consequences. Though most people in the Western world were neither genuine Christians nor well-schooled in philosophy, the public generally was strongly influenced by the teachings of the Christian faith and the thinking of those who followed in the Platonic tradition. The majority who lived wickedly either felt the need to justify their conduct or admitted they should be living differently.

Sad to say, however, the philosophy of naturalism with its denial of a personal God always has had its advocates. Agnostics, atheists, and pantheists, though differing from one another in many important respects, all agree that man is not to look beyond himself and the space-time world in his quest for ultimate truth. All concur in their denial of a personal God who has established absolute standards of right and wrong for mankind. They insist that man himself must determine truth and right conduct without reference to a God outside the universe. Denying a supernatural Authority they establish their own standards. The Greek hedonists made pleasure the criterion by which they determined their course of conduct. They did recognize that one might be forced to choose between momentary enjoyment or that which would provide gratification for a longer period of time, but all such determinations were made on selfish grounds. Another approach, called utilitarianism, declared that man must choose his course of conduct on the basis of a careful evaluation of what will provide the greatest good for the greatest number. This is basically the teaching of those who called themselves humanists, and of those modern theologians who advocate the "new morality." All of them deny a personal God who has established definite moral regulations for man to follow.

The denial of God and absolutes on the part of philosophers and theologians has been aided by the theory of naturalistic evolution. Most scientists today believe that man is the product of blind chance, and are determined to find the answers to their questions about life without reference to God. This pattern of thought has captured the majority of today's intellectuals, and increasing hostility toward the Christian faith is in evidence. Early naturalists like John Stuart Mill (1806 - 1873), a prominent utilitarian, did not deride Biblical standards of conduct or advocate cruel and immoral deeds. However, men like Nietzsche and Karl Marx were bitter in their hatred of the Scriptures. Today's naturalists for the most part have an extremely negative attitude toward the Bible, and are convinced that Christian virtues such as pity, sympathy, love, humility, and sexual purity are not always desirable. When one surveys the dialectical materialism of Marx, the pragmatism of John Dewey, the logical positivism of LeComte, or the existentialism of men like Sartre he sees that they differ from one another in many respects, but that they are all alike atheistic, and that each considers man to be the product of irrational causes, a creature upon whom no absolute moral code of conduct is binding. This is also the position of the "new morality" advocates. These men are often called theologians, but they do not believe in a living and personal God who has established standards of right and wrong.

The masses never keep pace with the intellectuals when a theoretical drift takes place. In Grecian history a period of time elapsed before the cynicism and despair of atheistic philosophers made their impact upon the life of the average Greek citizen. However, it is inevitable that the man on the street will eventually be influenced by the thought-streams of the intellectuals. The entire Greco-Roman civilization gradually abandoned the moral values of earlier days. Convinced that life had no significance or eternal reality, men and women plunged themselves into unspeakably degraded moral practices. Into this situation Jesus Christ came to illuminate the darkness of the age, to become the substitutionary sacrifice for sinners, and to deliver mankind from the power of sin and Satan. After His resurrection and ascension to Heaven, the apostolic preaching of Christ — crucified, risen, and coming again — transformed the lives of untold thousands.

In the years following the apostolic era, the Christian faith, along with the idealistic philosophy of Plato and Aristotle, continued to exert wide influence. The vast majority of mankind through the centuries held that the morals taught in the Bible constitute the good life. Almost everyone agreed that courage, truthfulness, kindness, and similar virtues should be practiced. Most people did not live Christian lives, but conceded that they should.

This attitude continued, even during the eighteenth and

nineteenth centuries, when a large number of influential religious leaders began to deny the inspiration of the Scriptures and to reject some New Testament doctrines. Leaders and people in the churches and in society still believed in God, immortality, and fixed moral standards. Men and women in general, even those who seldom attended church, agreed that people should be kind, truthful, honest and pure. The idea that God is a loving Heavenly Father who will eventually lead man into everlasting bliss was generally believed. No strong objective reasons could be given for this belief, but it was optimistically held almost everywhere.

A gradual change has been taking place during the last fifty years, however. Most people are not so confident that a good God really exists, but the majority of the adults in today's society do not permit themselves to think through the implications of the naturalistic philosophy of life they have tacitly accepted. They will agree that evolutionists perhaps are right, but maintain a certain amount of respect for religion, and entertain a vague hope for a blissful future after death. In everyday living, however, they have become practical atheists. They spend their time in a mad quest for happiness, turning to physical comforts and sensual pleasures. Though not advocating anarchy, they readily break the law if it provides material gain with only slight risk of detection. They are quite unconcerned for the needs of the underprivileged and the rights of the victims of human prejudice. They are trying to live in a halfway world between a hopeless atheism and a wishful belief in a loving, indulgent heavenly benefactor.

Many young people see the inconsistency and hypocrisy of this position. Some of them have genuine compassion for those who suffer as a result of radical bigotry and from an impersonal economic system. They are reacting against the crass materialism of their parents. They also reject all forms of religious belief. If no God exists, they say, it is useless to talk about moral principles. Therefore, they throw off all the restraints of religion, lose patience with the establishment, and sometimes become violently rebellious.

II. AUTHORITY — THE RATIONALE OF ITS RECOGNITION

Conditions in the world today reveal that neither young nor old can consistently put into practice the idea that man is nothing but a machine without purpose or significance. Among young people from age fifteen through nineteen the suicide rate has risen forty-eight percent in recent years. Nervous breakdowns and psychotic disorders are increasing at an alarming pace. The despair and frustration leading to these extreme reactions is compounded by glue-sniffing and the use of drugs, through pornography and outlandish sexual orgies. These young people do not know it, but in their conduct they are actually crying out for an authoritative voice to tell them who they are, why they are here, and what they must do.

Men still need the voice of authority. Even outside the realm of the Christian church there is a growing recognition that men are not mere animals, and that they cannot be satisfied with the utterly aimless and hopeless thinking of atheistic naturalism. A number of Europe's philosophers are following the lead of Ludwig Wittgenstein, an eminent German philosopher who possessed a brilliant mathematical and logical mind, and who felt that the secret to understanding mankind was to be found outside the space-time world. A sensitive person, he deeply longed for an authoritative external voice to speak to the moral needs of man, never realizing that his desire had already been met in the revealed Word of God.

Remember, scientists can only determine how things behave. They cannot find the answers to ultimate questions. If science were to become so advanced that men had a complete understanding of the physical world, it would still be unable to explain why the worlds exist, who man is, or where he is going. The Analytical Philosophy Movement, begun by Wittgenstein, is emphasizing the need for seriously studying the historical records and literary products of the past. These scholars say that such sources will give far more light upon the fundamental problems that face men than a study of the physical sciences. The implication of this trend is encouraging to the orthodox Christian, for it indicates that these men of learning recognize man's need to listen to a voice outside himself and the natural world. We unhesitatingly affirm that in the Scriptures we have that word of authority so essential to human welfare.

Historic Christianity has always contended that the Bible is inspired in a unique manner, and that it is therefore true and trustworthy in both its history and its teaching. The doctrine of the inspiration of the Scriptures has been confirmed in numerous ways. The manuscript copies have been subjected to scientific evaluation, and the authenticity of every book of the Bible has been maintained. Historical accuracy of the Scriptures has been repeatedly confirmed through archaeological evidence. The internal consistency of the sixty-six books, even though written over a period of some fifteen hundred years, is a source of amazement to all who carefully study the Bible. Furthermore, whenever men and women, boys and girls sincerely believe its message, trusting Jesus Christ as personal Lord and Savior, they are delivered from sin. Freedom from guilt, assurance of purpose, the experience of God's love — only these realities can meet the needs of today's restless, frustrated, despairing youth. These blessings are available to all who will listen to the authoritative voice of God as He speaks in the Scriptures. Who are you? Read God's Word and you will find out. How can you achieve true happiness? The answer can be found in the Bible. Where will you go after you die? The Word of God can give you the answer. No scientist or philosopher can speak with authority on these matters.

In these days of the so-called generation gap, society is divided into the young and into the old. We all find ourselves on one side or the other. But, the Bible — the most relevant book in all the world — meets the deepest needs of both young and old. More than 100 years ago a great theologian, speaking to his generation, expressed thoughts which are extremely appropriate to our age.

> Who can tell us whether this awful and mysterious silence, in which the Infinite One has wrapped himself, portends mercy or wrath? Who can say to the troubled conscience, whether He, whose laws in nature are inflexible and remorseless, will pardon sin? Who can answer the anxious inquiry whether the dying live on or whether they cease to be? Is there a future state? And if so, what is the nature of that untried condition of being? If there be immortal happiness, how can I attain it? If there be an everlasting woe, how can it be escaped? Let the reader close his Bible and ask himself seriously what he knows upon these momentous questions apart from its teachings. What solid foundation has he to rest upon in regard to

matters, which so absolutely transcend all earthly experience, and are so entirely out of the reach of our unassisted faculties? A man of facile faith may perhaps delude himself into the belief of what he wishes to believe. He may thus take upon trust God's unlimited mercy, his ready forgiveness of transgressors, and eternal happiness after death. But this is all a dream. He knows nothing, he can know nothing about it, except by direct revelation from heaven.

The question, therefore, is one of life or death. We will not, we can not give up our faith in the Bible. To do so is to surrender ourselves to blank despair. It is to blot out the sun from the heavens and extinguish at once the very source of light and life and holiness. "All flesh is as grass, and all the glory of man as the flower of grass. The grass withereth and the flower thereof falleth away; but the WORD OF THE LORD endureth forever." *

* Quoted from Olav Valen-Sendstad by J. W. Montgomery in *The Bible: the Living Word of Revelation* (Grand Rapids: Zondervan), pp. 217, 218.

13

THE PROBLEM OF FREEDOM

The majority of American citizens appreciate the four freedoms — speech, press, assembly, and religion — guaranteed by the Constitution. Never in history have these rights been put to the test as in the present generation. Purveyors of pornographic literature and producers of dirty movies constantly experiment to see how far they can go without arrest and conviction. Militant students deliberately invade the offices of school officials, and stage destructive riots and noisy demonstrations in the name of freedom. When a measure of restraint is placed upon them, they publicly declare that American freedom is a joke, and proclaim war against the establishment. They react this way in spite of the fact that the executive and judicial leaders of our day have shown more concern for the rights of minority groups and accused lawbreakers than any of their predecessors.

The problem is that the young activists who are raising a hue and cry about freedom do not understand the real meaning of the word. They confuse license with liberty, and are frustrated when their ungoverned way of life does not bring satisfaction. Even when they retreat from society to "do their own thing," they realize no true enjoyment. Deep depression may be seen on their faces, profound despondency is evidenced by the ever-increasing number of suicides, and utter desperation is shown in their daring use of dangerous drugs. These young people do not know the true answer to life's perplexing problems. They are completely bewildered when they try to answer questions concerning their identity, purpose, or destiny. Furthermore, they have nothing in which they can believe wholeheartedly. Their needs can be met, however, in the person of Jesus Christ, and thousands have found deliverance from sin and drug addiction when they turned to Him in faith. When He was here upon earth almost 2000 years ago, Jesus said to a group of His followers,

> . . . If ye continue in my word, then are ye my disciples indeed;
> And ye shall know the truth, and the truth shall make you free (John 8:31, 32).

Jesus promised true freedom to those who believe on Him. This liberty cannot be separated from the truth, and results in a responsible, productive life. Let's think about genuine freedom — its necessary condition, its basis, and its characteristics.

I. THE ESSENTIAL FOR TRUE FREEDOM

Real freedom begins when one believes on Jesus Christ. The Lord was speaking to those who trusted Him when He said, "And ye shall know the truth, and the truth shall make you free." *Believing* on Jesus Christ is a simple matter. Even children can exercise genuine faith at a tender age. In fact, the very simplicity of the Gospel has sometimes caused people to turn away. However, true faith in the Son of God brings most radical and revolutionary changes. One cannot exercise trust in the Savior without turning from sin and earnestly desiring to be delivered from its power. Believing on the Lord Jesus begins as a simple act of faith, but it leads to a truly transformed way of life.

Have you ever considered Jesus Christ? Most people who reject the Christian faith have not seriously confronted its claims. They have concluded that the Bible cannot be true because it speaks of miracles and the supernatural. Almost instinctively they have adopted the idea that a person should not believe anything that cannot be proved by scientific evaluation. They also assume that Christians can give no logical reason for their faith.

Believing on Jesus Christ does not contradict scientific evidence. The idea that one should not believe anything that cannot be proved scientifically is impossible to put into practice. An educated man in the field of science, for example, may talk against religion as something which is based upon faith and therefore unacceptable, but he himself cannot proceed in any scientific endeavor without assuming uniformity in nature and the existence of a causal relationship. These are assumptions that have validity because they work out in experience, but they are not scientifically demonstrable. The almost universal acceptance of the Law of Uniformity simply points out that every scientist must proceed upon some assumptions he accepts without prior proof.

The average person who rejects the Christian faith is also wrong in imagining that it is based upon blind belief or mere wishful thinking. The validity of Christianity rests upon undeniable evidence. The Bible is a unique book. Its historical accuracy is continually being attested by archaeological finds. The authenticity of the books of the Bible is clearly indicated as more and more manuscript copies are found. The evidence of the rapid growth of the first century Church is overwhelming. The enemies of the Christian faith have been unable to set forth good reasons for their rejection of these unquestionable facts. True, the Christian's faith in God does not rest upon a proved scientific formula, nor can the inspiration of Scripture be authenticated with such logical certainty that every unbeliever is compelled to accept it. However, when one reads the Scriptures, examines the evidence for their truthfulness, and then believes in the God revealed by them, he finds all his deepest needs fully met. He arrives at a satisfactory explanation of life, understands the problem of evil and the nature of man, and has the answer to the vexing questions concerning his purpose and destiny. Furthermore, he experiences the consciousness of sin forgiven and possesses a new power to be the kind of person he knows he ought to be. This is true freedom, and no person can possess it apart from faith in Jesus Christ.

II. THE BASIS FOR TRUE FREEDOM

The liberation Jesus promised to those who believe on Him is based upon truth. Christ told men that through faith they would know the ultimate verities of life. He thereby placed himself in sharp disagreement with those who take the nihilistic approach to truth and reality, denying the existence of God and a rational universe.

What did Jesus mean when He so confidently affirmed that men will arrive at truth only through faith in Himself? What is the TRUTH of which He spoke? In answer, we affirm

that Christ was speaking of "formulated revealed reality."
In the first place, Jesus said that TRUTH can be formulated,
expressed in words, and logically understood. It can be
stated systematically. This puts the words of Christ in direct contrast to the thinking of present-day existentialists,
for they think of truth as something irrational. The second
mark of TRUTH is that it has been *revealed*. The philosophers
of every age have been unable to find it through their own
efforts. No one person has a mind great enough to grasp
the truth, and no human being has ever been pure enough
to procure it through holy conduct. It only comes from
God. Finally, the TRUTH is concerned with *reality*. The fan-
tasy world of drug-induced hallucinations cannot be considered real.

God's truth has been revealed in the Bible. The Old Testament Scriptures declare His infinite power, His holy
nature, and His graciously condescending love and mercy.
They also unveil the secrets of the origin, nature, responsibility and destiny of man. From its sacred pages men can
know who they are, why they exist, what they must do,
and where they are going.

The supreme revelation of TRUTH came through Jesus
Christ. All the essential verities about God and man took
on a new dimension with the coming of Jesus Christ into
the world as recorded in the New Testament. The full
blaze of divine grace and glory was manifested in Him.
He came to interpret the nature of the holy and invisible
God to men alienated from Him because of sin. John declared,

> For the law was given by Moses, but grace and truth
> came by Jesus Christ.
> No man hath seen God at any time; the only begotten
> Son, who is in the bosom of the Father, he hath declared
> him (John 1:17, 18).

Through the incarnation, God made Himself tangible so
that men could understand Him. In the words and work of
Christ, God is made known to man.

God's TRUTH is not only revealed in the Bible and in
Christ, but it has also been verified in the historical Jesus.
He is not a mythical figure out of the shadowy past. His
appearance in Palestine nearly 2000 years ago changed the
course of history. Within a period of 20 years after His

death and resurrection, multiplied thousands affirmed their faith in Him, and the early Church became a factor with which the Roman Empire was forced to reckon. Commenting on the devices of unbelievers to explain away the preaching of the apostles and the phenomenal growth of the early Church, J. B. Phillips says, "It is surely straining credulity to bursting point to believe that this dramatic and sustained change of attitude was founded on hallucination, hysteria, or an ingenious swindle." * The revolutionary change in the apostles, and the enduring nature of their testimony in the face of bitter persecution, leaves no question regarding whether or not the earliest Christians believed in the literal resurrection of Christ. These first believers were so deeply convinced that Jesus had risen from the dead that no amount of opposition could shake their faith or cause them to renounce their allegiance to the Lord Jesus.

Furthermore, since the New Testament originated within the very century of the events it records and explains took place, no time-gap existed during which myths and legends could gradually overlay the truth. The abundant evidence from archaeology more and more establishes the early date of these New Testament books and confirms their historical accuracy. Therefore, those who insist that the true historical Christ cannot be known are inexcusably wrong.

Any sincere seeker after the truth is doing himself gross injustice if he does not seriously consider the Lord Jesus. Most people reject Him in ignorance, having never really investigated the claims of the Bible writers. If you earnestly desire the truth, you will prayerfully and diligently read the New Testament Scriptures, and you will discover that they are true. You will become personally acquainted with the living Christ they proclaim, and thereby understand who man is, why he is here, and how he can be delivered from the guilt and power of sin.

III. The Marks of True Freedom

Having shown that genuine freedom cannot be attained without the exercise of faith and the knowledge of truth, and having defined both faith and truth, we are now ready

* J. B. Phillips, *Your God Is Too Small* (New York: Macmillan), p. 112.

to consider freedom itself. When the Lord Jesus made His promise, "The truth shall make you free," what did He mean? What is this freedom Jesus promised? Is it liberty to live without regulatory principles, to carry into action every impulse, to gratify every lust? Our answer to these questions is an emphatic *no!* The freedom Jesus promised is not moral anarchy, a life without restraints of any kind. The teaching of the Bible and the lessons learned through human experience are in perfect harmony with one another, revealing that true freedom can be found only when one lives within the boundaries of law. A designer must obey certain natural principles to produce a truly beautiful and functional building or machine. An athlete must observe a number of health rules if he is to continue to perform well in strenuous activity over a period of years. Every field of worthwhile human endeavor involves obedience to certain disciplines.

In the moral realm no person is truly free who is plagued with deep feelings of guilt. Thousands of people annually visit clergymen, psychologists and psychiatrists, sensing their critical need for help. Deep feelings of guilt continually drive people both young and old into despair, which results in everything from sleeplessness to severe mental illness. He is not free who lives in such bondage.

The Bible teaches that the guilt of sin is not merely a mental illusion, but a reality to be faced and overcome. Sinful man is alienated from God by his wicked works, and is under condemnation. The apostle Paul declared that man's guilt with the resultant enmity against God is removed through the blood of Christ.

> And you, that were once alienated and enemies in your mind by wicked works, yet now hath he reconciled
> In the body of his flesh through death, to present you holy and unblamable and unreprovable in his sight (Colossians 1:21, 22).

Untold thousands, by trusting in Jesus Christ have experienced the joyous realization of forgiveness. The Son of God, as our Substitute, lived a sinless life and died on the cross to pay the price for our sins. When we believe on Him, God declares that the guilt of our sin is gone, the punishment already having been borne by this Savior.

In addition to the pressure of guilt, men also live in slavery to sin's power. True liberty consists in the ability to rationally consider all issues, understand them, recognize alternative possibilities of conduct, and then make a choice. The person who regularly drinks to excess is a slave, whether he knows it or not. The individual who pursues material gain as his goal finds himself lying, cheating, and becoming heartless in his attitude toward others. The thinking person who resolutely denies or ignores God is frustrated by the thought that life has no meaning or purpose, and either plunges himself into his occupation with such intensity that he becomes a slave, or he finds some other avenue by which he can express his deep anxiety. Some abandon all thought of personal dignity or worth, losing themselves in drink, drugs, and sensualism.

If you have never trusted Jesus Christ you need deliverance from the power of sin, for all who do not know Christ are its slaves. Paul speaks to believers concerning their former state of bondage, saying,

> For when ye were the servants of sin, ye were free from righteousness.
>   What fruit had ye then in those things of which ye are now ashamed? For the end of those things is death (Romans 6:20, 21).

Human experience confirms the Biblical teaching that iniquity enslaves its victims. True, all do not live in the depths of human depravity, nor does everyone gratify every lustful thought. However, no man can say he has achieved mastery over all his transgressions, evil habits, self-indulgences, or weaknesses. Freedom from the slavery of sin cannot be realized apart from Jesus Christ.

> Therefore, if any man be in Christ, he is a new creation; old things are passed away; behold, all things are become new (2 Corinthians 5:17).

Both past history and present experience indicate that true freedom and happiness are not obtained through giving rein to lust. The person who denies all moral standards, abandons all efforts to live decently, and gives free sway to his passions, will find himself hopelessly entwined in his sin. The only solution is to listen to the voice of God as He speaks in His Word. Remember, the books that make up our New Testament are not myths or legendary accounts written hundreds of years after the earthly life of Jesus. They are authentic and divinely inspired. Read them carefully and prayerfully. Be prepared for a drastic change in your way of life. But be assured that this new life will give you so much joy and rich freedom that you will never regret having become a servant of Jesus Christ.

14

THE PROBLEM OF HAPPINESS

What is happiness? This question, put to any audience, would receive a variety of replies. For some people, happiness is being on a golf course, for others it is a fishing trip, and for still others a new home. Some never think of happiness apart from bright lights, wild music, intoxicating beverages and sensual conduct. The word "happiness," you see, has many different meanings for people.

Mankind is seeking happiness with an intensity unrivaled in history, but the most optimistic must admit that man has not found it. Increasing suicides, frequent nervous breakdowns, and multiplied broken homes declare man's failure to attain happiness. On the other hand, those who have entered into a genuine relationship with Jesus Christ manifest an inner peace and radiant optimism which indicate they have discovered the secret of true joy. It will be helpful and interesting to consider today's futile quest for happiness, and then to discuss the only path to its achievement.

I. Man's Futile Quest for Happiness

Every person, young and old, desires happiness, but thousands have despaired of ever achieving it. They find their sentiments well expressed by a wealthy man, who, in response to a question concerning his own happiness, said, "Happy? Is anyone ever really happy?" People are trying to find satisfaction in many ways, but are unsuccessful because of a deep deficiency in their outlook on life.

The way many young people today seek happiness is quite disturbing to most adults. Of course, in every generation the young do things disapproved by their parents. However, wiser members of the older generation have always recognized that you cannot "put an old head upon young shoulders." Most young people today are not basically different from those of past generations, but a rather sizable minority are moving from one brief experience to another, continually looking for "kicks." For some, it is an act of extreme cruelty, for others, perverted sexual behavior; and, for still others, the performance of destructive deeds under the guise of battling the establishment.

While the majority do not behave like the militant activists, the average person today is seeking happiness apart from God. He outwardly professes to believe in the validity of moral laws, but does not have true faith. The tendency is to display a veneer of respectability while actually living selfishly and often immorally. Such a person may take a great deal of interest in his occupation and be active in social life, giving the impression of mental health and real happiness, and yet experience times of deep loneliness, ominous isolation, and vague emptiness.

The desperate futility many people feel in their quest for happiness is compounded by the condition of many homes. A large percentage of the youth have grown up in a troubled atmosphere, in homes either broken by divorce or under constant strain due to marital infidelity. Such young people may be surrounded by material benefits, but often feel unloved and unwanted. Furthermore, they are painfully aware that the outward impression of well-being on the part of their parents does not represent their true feeling. They have learned from observation of adults that a life which acknowledges the correctness of moral laws and puts on a mask of respectability, but has no deep inner convictions, produces only conflict and despair, not true happiness. These young people are sickened by the hypocrisy of such a life, and have decided to find enjoyment by openly denying and disregarding all thought of God and moral laws. However, they too are finding that the world of bright lights, wild music, and bizarre conduct leaves them lonely, unsatisfied, and depressed.

The underlying cause for the futility that has gripped many people who are seeking happiness is the result of a deep deficiency in their world and life view. Until recently, most folks were able to face life and enjoy it by convincing themselves that a good God lives in Heaven, and that everything will somehow work out well. When some cruel crime would be committed or if tragedy entered their lives, their faith would be shaken, but they would keep telling themselves that good would ultimately triumph over evil. Such a view of life is shallow, does not consider all of reality, and is not drawn from the holy Scriptures. It simply does not meet the needs of people in times of calamity, but it is better than the prevailing attitude current today. Most high school and college students are now taught that man is only a complex machine, the most highly developed product of blind evolution. Young people are therefore robbed of any concept of life as having meaning or purpose. No atheist has expressed the utter emptiness of life from the viewpoint of naturalism better than Bertrand Russell:

> That Man is the product of causes which had no prevision of the end they were achieving; that his origin, his growth, his hopes and fears, his loves and his beliefs, are but the outcome of accidental collocations of atoms; that no fire, no heroism, no intensity of thought and feeling, can preserve an individual life beyond the grave; that all the labors of the ages, all the devotion, all the inspiration, all the noonday brightness of human genius, are destined to extinction in the vast death of the solar system, and that the whole temple of Man's achievement must inevitably be buried beneath the debris of a universe in ruins — all these things, if not quite beyond dispute, are yet so nearly certain, that no philosophy which rejects them can hope to stand. *

Small wonder that an attitude of cynicism and despair grips people today, especially our youth! This explains why today's writers of books and plays are preoccupied with brutal murders, illicit love affairs, broken homes, unloved children, adultery, fornication, masochism, homosexuality, and prostitution. Many have concluded that if man is no more than the chance product of an irrational universe, then love, beauty, virtue, honesty, and loyalty are meaningless terms. Furthermore, if none of man's accomplishments will endure, why should he struggle and labor to produce anything worthwhile? This awful feeling of nothingness has been described as more unbearable than the thought of an eternal hell, and is driving people to suicide or madness.

* Bertrand Russell, *Mysticism and Logic* (New York: Barnes and Noble), p. 45.

Man is not a mere animal. He is depicted in the Bible as created in the image of God, and as a moral creature responsible to his Maker and Sustainer. Even apart from the testimony of Scripture, a person who thinks cannot help but realize that he is not a machine. He ponders the question of right and wrong, and wonders about death, eternity, and God. He could not do these things if he were the product of undirected force alone. He therefore instinctively feels his need of God, and knows that he ought to do better than he does. Furthermore, God made man to have fellowship with his Maker. The opening chapters of Genesis tell of Adam and Eve, Enoch, Noah, and Abraham walking with God. Naturalistic philosophy has failed to provide one of the deepest human needs — the instinctive desire to be loved and wanted. Tell a small child that you love him, or commend him upon some accomplishment, and watch his face beam with delight. Listen to the aged person, who has become helpless and bedridden, and whose children seldom visit him, as he speaks despairingly of the fact that no one needs him any longer. Think of the laborer who feels a new zest for his task when he is reminded that the small part he produces is vital to an important instrument in the space program. Every person needs a sense of personal identity and worth. This basic human need is denied by the prevailing naturalistic concept of man. Therefore, men will never be able to live happily without faith in God.

II. GOD'S PATH OF HAPPINESS

The Bible tells us how we can find happiness. It never enjoins its readers to seek earthly joys, but those who believe its message are of all men the most radiantly happy. This is because the Word of God contains the answers to life's vexing problems, and shows man how to live. The naturalist may insist that man is the product of evolution and therefore not a moral and rational being, but people in everyday life are constantly reasoning about things and making moral choices. The thinking person may decide to live as if beauty, love, and goodness are real, even though this is contrary to his naturalistic philosophy of life. But by so living, he declares that life is not subject to a rational explanation and admits his inability to be realistic. The only valid alternative is to believe that God exists, and to listen to what He says in His holy Word. The Christian faith alone presents a coherent explanation of the world and human life. The Bible depicts God in His infinite power and moral excellence, presents man as His special creation, and explains the presence of sin, suffering, and death in God's world. It also tells man how to be saved from his sin, and sets forth God's program for the future.

A vital ingredient in the recipe for happiness is the assurance of meaning. The Christian faith declares that man is not merely one among many species of animals, but he is a unique creation in the image and likeness of God. This is clearly declared in the creation story of Genesis 1 and 2, and is expressed poetically in Psalm 8.

> When I consider thy heavens, the work of thy fingers, the moon and stars, which thou hast ordained,
> What is man, that thou art mindful of him? And the son of man, that thou visitest him?
> For thou hast made him a little lower than the angels, and hast crowned him with glory and honor.
> Thou madest him to have dominion over the works of thy hands; thou hast put all things under his feet (Psalm 8:3-6).

As the Psalmist ponders the distant planets which move according to the ordinance of God, he marvels that the Lord should take any notice whatever of man. However, vast as the heavens are, brilliant as these radiant luminaries in the night skies may be, man, who seems to be so insignificant, is himself more grand and brilliant than any object of the universe. Though mortal and composed of earthly substance, God made him, God crowned him, and God gave him dominion. Thus man is at the same time a unique creature of great worth and a being who must be humble as he realizes that ultimately he is totally dependent upon the Lord.

This Biblical concept of man makes his performance in science, art, music and literature of great significance. He possesses God-given abilities, and therefore his accomplishments have eternal value. How different this view from that of Bertrand Russell and others, who see man only as the product of blind chance!

The Scriptures not only present humanity as the crown of God's creation, but also teach that each individual has worth — infinite value — in God's sight. This is revealed throughout the Old Testament. It portrays God constantly speaking to and through individuals, hearing their prayers and meeting their needs. The New Testament proclaims the same truth. The Lord Jesus showed God's compassion and concern for a weak and wandering sinner through His parables of the lost sheep, the lost coin and the lost son. He told of God's pleasure with the poor widow who could give only two mites, less than one-fifth of a cent in today's currency. He assured His followers that their Heavenly Father, who was concerned about a falling sparrow, who provided food for birds, and who gave beauty to the lily of the field, would care for them as well.

Not one person in the world stands outside the scope of God's love and tender mercy.

> For God so loved the world, that he gave his only be-gotten Son, that whosoever believeth in him should not perish, but have everlasting life (John 3:16).

Jesus Christ, the second person of the Trinity, became a human being that God might manifest Himself to man and redeem him from his sin. The Son came to this earth to reveal God, to live a perfect life as your substitute, and to die the death you deserve. If you have never believed on Him, you stand before God today as a sinner; but if you receive Jesus Christ you will become the recipient of ever-lasting life. Then, throughout all your days on earth and throughout eternity, you will know the thrilling reality of God's love for you.

When a person recognizes that he is not a mere accident and that his life has eternal meaning and significance, he will also conclude that he is a free moral agent who is re-sponsible for his own behavior. Man needs this recognition of responsibility if he is to be truly happy. The tendency of many psychologists in recent years to look upon a person as nothing more than a computer, whose every word and act is merely a conditioned response to chemical or environ-mental stimuli, destroys man's self-respect. It is also un-realistic, and produces disastrous consequences in many lives. The Bible holds man accountable for his sin. It ex-plicitly commands the right and forbids the wrong, and declares,

> Be not deceived, God is not mocked, for whatever a man
> soweth, that shall he also reap (Galatians 6:7).

Men sin because they choose to do so, not because God in any way forces their wills. In fact, mankind has sold itself into the slavery of sin, and in human strength alone no person is able to lift himself from his sinful state. Jeremiah says,

> Can the Ethiopian change his skin, or the leopard his
> spots? Then may ye also do good, that are accustomed
> to do evil (Jeremiah 13:23).

However, though man is willfully depraved and cannot transform himself into a righteous person by his own efforts, the Bible makes it clear that he is not a mere robot. Every normal individual possesses a genuine personality as a morally responsible being. True, he cannot save himself, but he can receive God's salvation as a free gift. Whenever an individual acknowledges his sin, believes the message concerning Jesus Christ, and then by an act of the will places his trust in the Lord Jesus, God forgives his sin, imparts a new life, and leads him to final victory. With this new life and the indwelling Holy Spirit the believer is now able to exercise self-control and self-denial. These disciplines are good, putting sinews into the personality. They help a person gain mastery of self, and with that to acquire poise and strength.

The Biblical guidelines are sometimes called repressive, and many non-Christian psychologists frown upon the prohibitions and regulations found in the Bible. They think it is better to deny that wrong drives are present, thus closing the mind to real problems rather than facing and overcoming them. Experience has demonstrated the correctness of the Bible approach. No one can really achieve happiness without recognizing his own integrity as a person. This is true because God made man in His own image — a personality possessing a mind, will, and emotions. Thousands can testify that they never knew real spiritual joy until they realized that Christ loved them and responded to His invitation,

> Come unto me, all ye that labor and are heavy laden,
> and I will give you rest.
> Take my yoke upon you, and learn of me; for I am

meek and lowly in heart, and ye shall find rest unto your souls.

For my yoke is easy, and my burden is light (Matthew 11:28-30).

After a person has discovered that life is meaningful, that he is a responsible moral agent, and deliberately places his faith in Jesus Christ, he experiences the assurance of forgiveness and gains a glorious hope for the future. Man cannot be truly happy without hope. A famous European declared that in his psychological analysis tests he discovered that every person over thirty-five consciously or unconsciously avers that he is dominated by the fear of death and the problem of religion. People who believe that everything ends at the grave may decide to live a relatively good life, but they surely cannot be happy. Life is full of uncertainties, and sooner or later our loved ones must leave us, or we must take our departure from them. If the future holds forth only the prospect of everlasting nothingness, life mocks man. If that were the case, we would have, as someone said, "the endowments of a god and the career of an insect." The glorious message of the Gospel is one of supreme hope.

The resurrection of Jesus Christ was the subject of apostolic preaching because they saw in it the prophecy and pledge of their own resurrection from the grave. The early Christians were filled with hope as they anticipated the future. This same certainty was the source of joy and strength for the Christian martyrs during the time of bitter persecution which followed the apostolic age. On the walls of the Roman catacombs where the believers had been driven, they scrawled one word, *vita*, meaning "life." They knew they possessed eternal life, and not even the horrors of the arena could dispel their joy.

How precious the Christian's hope! Some people spend all their years in poverty or pain, but their knowledge of Christ has given them the assurance of a glorious eternity. All the suffering of this present life will be as nothing when compared to the glory we shall enjoy. That loved one who died in Christ has left for only a little while. Take comfort! Rejoice! Someday we must all leave this earth. It may be while the glow of childhood is still on our cheeks, or in the noonday of life, or even when the shadows have lengthened. Death for the Christian, however, is not an enemy to be feared, for hand-in-hand with Jesus we will go with unfaltering feet and trusting heart through the valley of the shadow, and with hope-encircled brow we will enter the land of fadeless day and unending joy. Christ gives life meaning, dignity, and hope.

Part III

HAPPINESS IN

SPITE OF ADVERSITY

15

HAVE FAITH IN GOD

The Radio Bible Class reaches thousands of aged people who are ill or feeble, many in hospitals or convalescent homes where they will live out the remainder of their earthly days. Its ministry also touches the lives of a great number of younger people who are afflicted in one way or another. Many listeners write to tell us that they spend their days and nights under the burden of crushing sorrow or bitter disappointment. Some who are not personally involved in great suffering or anguish are nevertheless troubled when they reflect upon the misery and heartache of others all about them. They say it is hard to believe that a loving, wise, and all-powerful God is really in charge of the universe. We receive numerous letters from despairing people who express doubts about God, and ask us to tell them why there is so much pain and sorrow in the world. On the other hand, every week hundreds write of the joy they have found in the midst of suffering, and of their thankfulness even under the most adverse circumstances. Their letters glow with the light of God's grace, and are an encouragement to us as we read them.

In this chapter we will emphasize the need for faith in God. If you are plagued by sorrow, pain, or heartache, you should reflect upon God as He is revealed in the Bible. Don't harbor doubts about His existence. The fact that you are a thinking being who lives in an ordered universe gives witness to the Lord's power and wisdom. Deep in your heart you know you are more than an accident of nature. Furthermore, you can rely upon the authenticity of the Bible. Every sincere seeker after God and truth who has investigated the evidence will affirm that the New Testament documents must be accepted as reliable records. The Bible is proven to be God's Word, and declares that He is good, affirms His infinite wisdom and power, and gives abundant evidence of His absolute integrity.

I. GOD'S GOODNESS IS VERIFIABLE

The apostle John tells us that "God is love" (1 John 4:8). Don't allow your own subjective thoughts or the bitter comments of unbelieving people to shake your confidence in God's goodness. Those who deny the existence of a holy and loving Heavenly Father have permitted themselves to be blinded by Satan or swayed by their feelings. God's love, mercy, and grace are apparent to all who are willing to see them.

The created world reflects God's love. The spiritually discerning person feels a sense of gratitude whenever he sees orchards blooming in the springtime or heavy with fruit in the fall. He cannot observe the sunset with its gorgeous colors, the ocean surging and sparkling beneath the sun, or mountains rising to their majestic, snow-capped heights without thinking of God and the variety of loveliness He has provided. Even God's care for animals shows His kindness, for the Psalmist declared,

> The eyes of all wait upon thee; and thou givest them their food in due season.
> Thou openest thine hand, and satisfiest the desire of every living thing (Psalm 145:15, 16).

God's treatment of unsaved mankind also speaks of His love. He sends sunshine and rain, helps men in time of need, and provides many riches for all to enjoy. He has ordained marriage and the family which are good. The beauties of nature, art, literature, and music are given by God for man's enrichment. Paul told the heathen citizens of Lystra that God had been speaking to them even before they had heard the Gospel,

> . . . in that he did good, and gave us rain from heaven, and fruitful seasons, filling our hearts with food and gladness (Acts 14:17).

The war and violence, brutality and barbarism, inequality and suffering around us are real, but they do not disprove God's love. They are here because man has rebelled against his Maker and is living wickedly and selfishly. Even the eruptions of nature in violent earthquakes or turbulent hurricanes do not deny God's kindness, but they take place because the earth itself is under the curse of sin. Don't let suffering or heartache distort your perspective on life. The world is still filled with beautiful sights and sounds, laughing children, and happy homes. The God who made this world is good indeed, and has planned a glorious eternity for all who trust Him.

God's love is also manifested in His mercy and grace. He is patient with His children, forgiving and blessing them even when they fail again and again. He is longsuffering to the ungodly. Men may ignore Him, blaspheme His name, ridicule His Book, malign His servants, and break His moral laws, but the Lord in mercy withholds the judgment He could righteously rain down upon them. Furthermore, God has made known His grace to all men. He cannot approve of sin or violate His holiness by allowing it to go unpunished, but in love He has provided salvation in the person of Jesus Christ.

> For God so loved the world, that he gave his only begotten Son, that whosoever believeth in him should not perish, but have everlasting life (John 3:16).

Christian friend, how can you doubt God's love, mercy, and grace? Were it not for His love, Christ would never have come to bring salvation and give you hope. If it were not for God's mercy, no one would have ever experienced happiness through the joyful laughter of children, the tenderness of family ties, the joy of Christian fellowship, or the anticipation of Heaven. But thousands upon thousands have been able to give ringing testimonies of the peace and gladness Jesus Christ has given them.

When you are suffering, you must remember that it is only a small part of the total picture. Think of the evidences of God's goodness around you, and reflect upon the glory that awaits you. Resist the desire to think only of yourself and your situation. The apostle Paul said,

> For I reckon that the sufferings of this present time are not worthy to be compared with the glory which shall be revealed in us (Romans 8:18).

Paul was viewing his life from the perspective of eternity. He looked beyond this troubled world and was convinced that the glory which awaited him was so much greater than the pain he endured in this life that comparison was impossible. If Paul could say this, so can you, for your situation could be no worse than his. He suffered "a thorn in the flesh" (2 Corinthians 12), thought by many to be a painful eye disease. He had been imprisoned, beaten, shipwrecked, and stoned. In addition, stubborn and violent critics accused him of fickleness, of self-laudation, of assumption of authority, of being contemptible in appearance, and of being hypercritical and cowardly. He knew loneliness, pain, and the frustration of being misunderstood and hated, but he triumphed over all these obstacles because he never doubted God's goodness.

II. God's Power and Wisdom Have Been Demonstrated

After reminding yourself of God's goodness, reflect upon His wisdom and power. The Bible presents Him as the One who knows everything, and is wise beyond human comprehension. Paul declared,

> Oh, the depth of the riches both of the wisdom and knowledge of God! How unsearchable are his judgments, and his ways past finding out!
> For who hath known the mind of the Lord? Or who hath been his counselor?
> Or who hath first given to him, and it shall be recompensed unto him again?
> For of him, and through him, and to him, are all things: to whom be glory forever. Amen (Romans 11:33-36).

The book of Revelation speaks of Him as the "Almighty Lord" nine times, and the Scriptures repeatedly affirm the truth declared by Job when he said, "I know that thou canst do everything, and that no thought can be withheld from thee" (Job 42:2). God is so powerful that He created angels and man as free moral agents, and dared to give them the choice of obeying or disobeying Him. He knew nothing would happen that He couldn't control. Satan and a large company of angelic beings rebelled against the Lord, were expelled from Heaven, and still exert awesome power today, for God allows them a great deal of freedom. But the Lord remains in ultimate sovereignty. The Bible declares that finally, as time merges into eternity, Satan and all the wicked who have followed him will be cast into the lake of fire (Revelation 20:11-15). The redeemed of all ages will inherit the new heavens and new earth (Revelation 21 and 22), for God's wise decrees will be carried out.

I know there are times in the lives of some Christians when they find it hard to believe in a God who is infinite in wisdom and power. Many wrongs seem to go unpunished, many prayers appear to go unanswered, and much of the suffering about us looks so senseless that one is sometimes tempted to wonder where God is and why He permits things to be this way. But in this sinful, troubled, and mixed-up world we can still affirm our faith in God's wisdom and power! He temporarily permits evil men and the rulers of darkness to have their day, but He has not for one moment lost absolute authority over His universe. Men may rise in brazen impudence and say that God is dead, may rebel against His laws and declare themselves masters of their own destiny, but they cannot disturb His serenity. The Lord has but to speak a word, and the puny little creatures who defy Him will perish. The Psalmist, after describing the fury of rebellion by the nations against God and His Christ, declares,

> He who sitteth in the heavens shall laugh; the Lord shall have them in derision.
> Then shall he speak unto them in his wrath, and vex them in his great displeasure (Psalm 2:4, 5).

This God, who remains calm and peaceful in the midst of oppression and violence, also has control of every aspect of your life and mine. He knows us, and is aware of our limits, and will never allow us to be tested beyond the measure of His grace and our ability. The days may become dreary, the nights long and dark, but God's grace will always be sufficient for any test. When He says it is enough, the period of trial will end.

Christian friend, do you daily remind yourself of God's wisdom and power? Have you looked up and declared, "From everlasting to everlasting thou art God"? Have you recently read the accounts which depict the Lord Jesus casting out demons, healing the sick, stilling the tempest, and conquering death? Has your inner being thrilled at the thought, "Jesus Christ is the same yesterday, today, and forever"? You may not be able to understand why life takes the turn it does; you may be perplexed as you contemplate the rise and fall of nations; you may not be able to answer critics who ask you to explain the seeming triumphs of wrong over right, but you can look up and say with Job, "I know that my redeemer liveth."

Read the Bible and focus your attention upon the God it reveals. He is too good to be cruel, too wise ever to do wrong, and too powerful to be defeated. His plans have been conceived in love and wisdom, and His power is your guarantee that His good purposes will be realized.

III. God's Promises Are Sure

In addition to its wonderful revelation of God's love, wisdom, and power, the Bible contains many divine promises for our comfort and strength. We can rely upon what God says. Since He is both holy and all-powerful, He never lies. Read carefully the promises He has given in His Word and allow them to make an impact upon your life. Both the Old and New Testaments are rich in His assurance of love and purpose. Even the promises He made to Israel have an application for you. If you are suffering, take to your own heart the well-known words of Isaiah,

> When thou passeth through the waters, I will be with thee; and through the rivers, they shall not overflow thee; when thou walkest through the fire, thou shalt not be burned, neither shall the same kindle upon thee (Isaiah 43:2).

This promise of God's presence is as much for you personally as it was for Israel. He will accompany every step of your journey, and not permit any real harm to come into your life. When you face the prospect of a trial you think will be greater than you can bear, take comfort in God's message to Paul when he asked that his "thorn in the flesh" might be removed,

> And he said unto me, My grace is sufficient for thee; for my strength is made perfect in weakness . . . (2 Corinthians 12:9).

The Lord will give you sufficient grace for every test. Believe this promise, and you will be able to say a hearty "Amen" as you read the remainder of this verse, "Most gladly, therefore, will I rather glory in my infirmities, that the power of Christ may rest upon me."

When you are ill, and have no assurance that you will be well again, meditate upon these words of the Psalmist:

> The Lord will strengthen him upon the bed of languishing; thou wilt make all his bed in his sickness (Psalm 41:3).

When death comes into your home, or when you realize that you must soon take your journey through the valley of the shadow, comfort yourself with the words of Jesus:

> Let not your heart be troubled; ye believe in God, believe also in me.
>
> In my Father's house are many mansions; if it were not so, I would have told you. I go to prepare a place for you.
>
> And if I go and prepare a place for you, I will come again, and receive you unto myself, that where I am, there ye may be also (John 14:1-3).

Perhaps you need encouragement because, though you are sure of Heaven, you somehow are afraid of dying. Think of Christ's beautiful words to Martha:

> . . . I am the resurrection, and the life; he that believeth in me, though he were dead, yet shall he live.
>
> And whosoever liveth and believeth in me shall never die . . . (John 11:25, 26).

Christian friend, you will not have to endure the worst aspect of death. You will never experience the desolation and darkness that comes upon the one who doesn't know Jesus Christ. For you, death has lost its terror and sting. Jesus said that you will not die in the fullness of what death is — separation from God. If you know Christ, dying will come not as a monster to be feared, but as a messenger from Heaven. It will close your eyes, kiss away your breath, and place your hand in that of Jesus Christ. The Lord Himself will lead you, and you will go through the waters with unfaltering feet, a trusting heart, and a hope-encircled brow to rise again in the land called Glory. You will forever dwell in that country John described when he said,

> And God shall wipe away all tears from their eyes; and there shall be no more death, neither sorrow, nor crying,

neither shall there be any more pain; for the former things are passed away (Revelation 21:4).

Child of God, even the most heavy burdens and difficult trials of life need not defeat you. God has given you His Holy Spirit to indwell you, His Word to speak to you, and a glorious, wonderful hope. Set your thoughts upon Him and His perfections. Read and believe His promises, and you will find life to be good. You will be marked by a holy optimism and a fullness of joy that honors God. You will be among those happy saints who have been able to "glory in tribulation," and your life will be a help to all who know you.

16

WILLING SUBMISSION

It isn't hard to be happy when all is going well. When one has enough money, good health, and friends, he usually doesn't worry about the future. Many people are completely unprepared, therefore, for adversity when it comes into their lives. One cannot know when some great disaster will come, or how he will react when it does. Imagine the couple who just received news that their precious child has an illness which will soon prove fatal. That young mother buries her head in her husband's arms and sobs, "Why?" Life looks far different to these two people than it did just the day before. Another man is informed that the malignant condition for which he was treated is recurring, and that the doctors can do very little for him. He is too young to die, but his case is hopeless. Life looks very dark to him today. Many others have serious problems — unemployment, insecurity, a retarded or crippled child, or a chronic illness.

If any of these terms describe your situation right now, you must ask yourself, "How can I cope with my problems?" You know that trying to drown your grief through excessive drinking or in a mad pursuit of pleasure is not the solution. If you rebel and become bitter, you will ultimately sink into hopeless despair, concluding that if God exists, He is either unwilling or unable to help you. Any of these reactions is an indication that you haven't learned how to live with adversity.

In this chapter we will show that a Christian can live triumphantly even in the most adverse circumstances of life. He knows that the Lord is a good, all-powerful, and infinitely wise God. He is confident that God has a loving purpose for his life, and that suffering is part of a program which will lead to his ultimate welfare. He believes the Bible is

God's Word, and familiarizes himself with its teaching about affliction in the life of a Christian. He accepts its instruction as true, avoids the pitfalls against which he is warned, and obeys the admonition to exercise his faith.

I. BELIEVING THE BIBLICAL INSTRUCTIONS

The Bible makes it clear that the Lord permits adversity to enter the lives of His people for the purpose of chastening. The writer of Hebrews declares,

> . . . My son, despise not thou the chastening of the Lord, nor faint when thou art rebuked of him;
>
> For whom the Lord loveth he chasteneth, and scourgeth every son whom he receiveth.
>
> If ye endure chastening, God dealeth with you as with sons; for what son is he whom the father chasteneth not?
>
> But if ye be without chastisement, of which all are partakers, then are ye bastards, and not sons.
>
> Furthermore, we have had fathers of our flesh who corrected us, and we gave them reverence. Shall we not much rather be in subjection unto the Father of spirits, and live?
>
> For they verily for a few days chastened us after their own pleasure, but he for our profit, that we might be partakers of his holiness (Hebrews 12:5-10).

The Greek word rendered "chastening" refers to discipline and reproof in the training of a child. This passage of Scripture tells us the trials that come into the life of a believer are tokens of God's concern for him. People who do not know the Lord suffer too, but their afflictions come as the result of their own sin or simply because they are members of the human family which is under Adam's curse. If you are a child of God, however, you have the assurance that affliction is part of God's wise plan for your life. In fact, you may look upon adversity as proof that you really belong to the Lord (Hebrews 12:7), and you may be certain that it is designed for your good (Hebrews 12:10). You see, a father disciplines his own child because he loves him and is thinking of his future. This human parent may sometimes act hastily or be mistaken, but he is motivated by love. Similarly, God our Heavenly Father chastens only those who belong to Him that they might be refined and purified. The certainty of God's loving purpose in testing prompted Paul to write the Christians in Rome,

. . . we glory in tribulations also, knowing that tribulation worketh patience;

And patience, experience; and experience, hope;

And hope maketh not ashamed, because the love of God is shed abroad in our hearts by the Holy Spirit who is given unto us (Romans 5:3-5).

Believers may be subjected to the pressures of poverty, sorrow, persecution, pain, and loneliness, but they are able to rejoice in them. As a believer who walks close to God undergoes adversity he develops patience; not mere passive endurance, but an attitude of mind which enables him actually to overcome and conquer the trials of life. This quality enabled Paul and Silas to sing praises while confined in prison, their feet held by stocks and their backs bruised and bleeding. When the early Christians were thrown to wild beasts in the arena, their persecutors saw more than merely the numb silence of victims resigned to the inevitable, but observed a radiant optimism which defied explanation. Their faith triumphed over affliction.

Christian friend, I am not trying to tell you that your lot in life is easy. I am not minimizing the pain, the heartbreak, or the disappointment you must endure, for I know such experiences are difficult. But, on the other hand, I also am certain that the Word of God is true, and that God's ultimate aim is to give you a glorious eternity in Heaven. Read the Bible and believe what it says. God will enable you to soar above your circumstances and reap the benefit from your trials.

II. Obeying God's Admonitions

Many Christians, however, have not profited through affliction. They endure a series of difficulties without a strengthening of faith, a deepening of love, or a growing in holiness. You see, hardship and testing do not automatically bring about spiritual growth. God's chastening provides great benefits only "unto them who are exercised by it" (Hebrews 12:11). The believer must resolutely avoid Satan's pitfalls and learn to exercise faith if his suffering is not to be wasted.

Satan, that great enemy of God and man, is infuriated by Christians whose lives bring glory to God. He would much rather see a believer defeated by life's trials and difficulties.

We must guard against attitudes which will bring Satan delight. We must be alert to three of the most common foes of a radiant Christian testimony: gloomy endurance, whining self-pity, and bitter resentment.

If you see your suffering as nothing more than the out-working of a fixed decree, something to be endured with grim determination and raw courage, you'll never receive the blessings God has for you. In fact, you will become morose and gloomy, even though you are a Christian. True, you may not be expressing yourself in bitter words of un-belief, but neither are you demonstrating that you really love Him, and that you believe He loves you. Therefore, don't be satisfied with mere resignation to the inevitable. Tell the Lord that you know His chastening is grounded in His love and wisdom, and that it is for your eternal welfare. Dwell upon this truth in your thinking until it gets hold of you, until you can actually thank God for it.

Another mistake to avoid is self-pity. Don't entertain the thought — not even for one moment — that your situation is worse than that of anyone else. Instead of feeling sorry for yourself, think of others who have trials greater than yours. Things could be much worse, and you still have many rea-sons to be thankful. Numerous believers have triumphed over seemingly impossible difficulties, and that grace of God which gave them strength is also available to you. Read the book of Job. Review Paul's account of the suf-fering he endured as recorded in 2 Corinthians 11, and then think of his words, "For I reckon that the sufferings of this present time are not worthy to be compared with the glory which shall be revealed in us" (Romans 8:18). Reflect upon what Christ suffered for your salvation. You'll never need to go through the agony He experienced. Re-member, many have suffered far more than you without complaint or self-pity.

A third error you must shun is resentment toward God. Keep from viewing your suffering as punishment. The un-saved are punished: the believer is chastened. Don't think of God as vindictive or cruel. Never ask the question, "What have I done to deserve this kind of treatment?" God is not punishing you. Jesus paid the full price for your sins, and what you are enduring is chastening. Your Heav-enly Father is dealing with you in love to bring correction to your life. Be on guard against any thought, therefore, which might suggest that you do not trust God to do what's right.

The child of God can best avoid Satan's pitfalls in a season of affliction by exercising his faith in God. Trouble will afterward yield "the peaceable fruit of righteousness unto them who are exercised by it" (Hebrews 12:11). You must act positively in times of suffering by earnest self-examination, and then by making the necessary adjustments in your life.

By searching your heart you will be able to discover whether or not something needs correction. Remember, not every affliction is the result of specific sin. When it is, how-ever, the Holy Spirit will let you know. The Lord some-times chastens that you may be restored, and He will reveal the particular weakness or fault in your life. Read the Word of God, examine your heart, and pray. How about your thought life? Are you covetous, envious, hateful, or lust-ful? Maybe you need a lesson in humility. Perhaps you are trying to do everything in your own strength, and you need to learn dependence upon the Lord. It is even possible that you are so selfish you hardly ever pray for others. God may be seeking to remedy this condition. I can assure you that if you will honestly and sincerely read the Bible, search your heart, and seek God's face, the Spirit of truth will show you your weaknesses, errors, and sins.

If the affliction that has come into your life is not de-signed to correct some specific fault or sin, but is simply a means of teaching you patience or producing Christlike-ness, the Holy Spirit will show you. Never underestimate His illuminating ministry. Look to Him daily in faith. He will give you the information you need to receive the in-tended blessing.

When you learn the reason for your suffering, take im-mediate steps to make right what is wrong. You can over-come sin, not in your own strength, of course, but in the power of God. Begin by humbly looking to Him, for He "giveth more grace." James declares, "God resisteth the proud, but giveth grace unto the humble" (James 4:6). The Lord is available, not to proud, self-sufficient persons, but to those who are humble and look to Him.

Take time to study your Bible and pray. Ask the Lord for grace to overcome your pride, your self-will, or your worldliness. Your Heavenly Father wants you to be Christ-like; He is interested in purifying your character, and He will work to this end. My father used to say that this cleansing could be accomplished in three ways: "the gentle way, the severe way, and the extreme way."

The "gentle way" is by confessions of sins, which of course includes a sincere desire to be delivered from their power. The apostle John assured us that "If we confess our sins, he is faithful and just to forgive us our sins, and to cleanse us from all unrighteousness" (1 John 1:9).

The "severe way" is necessary when we refuse to confess. God must then chasten, sometimes by sending bitter trials into our lives. Paul told the Corinthian Christians that many people in the church suffered physical affliction because of abuses in connection with the Lord's table (1 Corinthians 11:30).

The "extreme method" is chastening by the untimely death of the believer; he does not forfeit salvation, but he will suffer loss at the judgment seat of Christ. In the same verse that Paul spoke of weaknesses and sicknesses, he said that "many sleep" (1 Corinthians 11:30). Sometimes it is better for a Christian to be taken out of this world than remain here to practice wickedness. Since this is true, you should deal with sin when the Holy Spirit reveals it to you. Confess it, submit yourself to God, resist the devil, and the Lord will give you victory.

Christian friend, have you learned how to live with adversity? Are you able to find reason for thanksgiving even when everything seems to be going against you? Do you really believe what the Bible says about testings and trials? Are you growing in Christlikeness through the afflictions of life? Remember, everything God permits has its source in His wisdom and love, and is aimed at your eternal welfare. He knows what is best for you. This confidence will deliver you from gloomy endurance, whining self-pity, and a rebellious spirit. It will lift you to new heights of spiritual joy. It has worked in the lives of others, and it will in yours as well.

A few years ago, a Christian family lost the eldest of their two daughters in a tragic accident. Then, about a year later, these parents were told that their second lovely teenager had an incurable heart condition which would soon take her life. But they didn't despair. They didn't complain that God was unfair or whimper in self-pity. Instead, through tear-filled eyes they said, "Lord, not my will, but Yours be done." They didn't understand why God would take both of their girls, but they knew the truth of these words from Isaiah,

> For my thoughts are not your thoughts, neither are your ways my ways, saith the Lord.
> For as the heavens are higher than the earth, so are my ways higher than your ways, and my thoughts than your thoughts (Isaiah 55:8, 9).

They believed that God had good reason for permitting these great sorrows to come into their lives, and were assured that someday they would understand. This husband and wife were also strengthened by the confidence that they would meet their daughters again in Heaven. Their victorious attitude was the means of blessing to all those with whom they came in contact. What a testimonial to the grace of God! This grace is available to you. With God's help you can be triumphant, even though you live with adversity.

17

GOD'S LAW OF LIFE

We live in a broken world. My father, Dr. M. R. De-Haan, once pointed out that sin has brought disruption into life, and that from the earliest days of consciousness we live in a world of broken things: the infant cries over a broken toy, the child over a broken sled, and the young person over a broken promise. Parents sometimes weep over the untimely death of a child or the waywardness of a grown son or daughter. Many husbands or wives shed tears over an unfaithful mate and the resulting broken home. In fact, everyone who reaches maturity knows to some extent the agony of bereavement, the frustration of failing health, and the disappointment of shattered dreams. No one can live in this world without sharing some of the heartbreak that is part of life. Greed, cruelty, and deceitfulness on the part of our fellowmen, plus the gradual departure of loved ones and friends as the advancing years take their toll, fill our lives with broken things.

The Bible tells us how to live victoriously with the inevitable distresses of life. The Christian who lives in obedience to the Word of God doesn't have to retreat to an unreal world and refuse to face life as it is. Nor will he find it necessary to stoically accept the bitter with the sweet. He need not become sour in his outlook, but can be a radiant testimony to the sufficiency of God's grace. To do this, he must acknowledge the divine law of life as set forth by the Lord Jesus, who declared that a new, abundant, and fruitful life cannot be realized without a death:

> Verily, verily, I say unto you, Except a grain of wheat fall into the ground and die, it abideth alone; but if it die, it bringeth forth much fruit.
>
> He that loveth his life shall lose it; and he that hateth his life in this world shall keep it unto life eternal.

> If any man serve me, let him follow me; and where
> I am, there shall also my servant be: if any man serve
> me, him will my Father honor (John 12:24-26).

Our Lord spoke these words shortly before He went to the
cross, where He would give His life to reap a harvest of
redeemed men and women. His atoning death — not His
worthy example or noble teaching — has now become the
means by which sinners are forgiven and transformed. The
Lord Jesus willingly gave Himself to the accursed death on
the cross that He might be our Savior. He did not think of
Himself, but of us. The same principle that motivated the
Lord Jesus must be applied in our lives, because "as he is,
so are we in this world" (1 John 4:17). For us, too, the path
to life and fruitfulness is through dying to self. Only as we
submit to the "law of the cross" will we reap a full harvest
of blessing. This law demands that we yield ourselves to
God, and that we actively seek to overcome the evils of our
selfish nature.

I. Humble Submission to God

The first step toward victory over tragedy is to acknowledge God's right to use us for His glory in whatever way
He sees fit. After all, if we are Christians, we belong to
Him. When we submit to Him, we will find consolation in
suffering and strength to endure persecution for Christ's
sake.

Submission brings consolation in suffering. How thrilling
to know we are Christ's special possession! The Lord was
talking about you, dear Christian, when He said,

> My sheep hear my voice, and I know them, and they
> follow me.
> And I give unto them eternal life; and they shall
> never perish, neither shall any man pluck them out of
> my hand (John 10:27, 28).

The Lord Jesus knows you as an individual. You are precious to Him, and He will see you safely to Heaven. What
a consolation! But you can only experience the reality of
this assurance if you live under "the law of the cross." As
long as you insist upon living your own life, refusing to
acknowledge Jesus Christ as your Lord, you will miss the
comfort that comes to those who gladly assert they belong
to God completely. If the truth that you are Christ's pos-

session takes hold of your life, you will find consolation and strength through suffering. Remember, you have been purchased by the blood of Christ. On your part this truth calls for complete submission. On God's part, He has pledged never to let you go. You may be worthless in your own eyes, and even wonder why God ever cared for you, but if you yield completely to Him, you can rejoice in the fact that He has proved His love for you. Living in a broken world you can experience happiness through suffering when you heed the words of the Lord Jesus, "He that loveth his life shall lose it; and he that hateth his life in this world shall keep it unto life eternal" (John 12:25).

Submission results in strength to face persecution. When a person willingly participates in God's law of life and makes it his aim to please the Lord, he places himself in a position the world simply cannot understand. Unregenerate man says, "Assert yourself!" "Develop self-confidence!" "Get rid of guilt feelings!" and "Enjoy yourself!" The Christian, however, has identified with Him who said that true happiness comes to those who are poor in spirit, meek, merciful, pure in heart; to people who mourn, hunger and thirst after righteousness, and who are persecuted for Christ's sake (Matthew 5:1-12). No wonder Jesus warned His disciples about the world's hatred, saying,

> If the world hate you, ye know that it hated me before it hated you.
> If ye were of the world, the world would love its own; but because ye are not of the world, but I have chosen you out of the world, therefore the world hateth you (John 15:18, 19).

When you are misunderstood, ridiculed, or persecuted, remember that you are an alien in this world. Your values are different, and so are your standards. The natural man is often antagonized by your adherence to Christian ethics. Your departure from the world's view of life is a rebuke to him, because your commitment to Christ is a declaration that manmade materialism and philosophy cannot give you peace and joy. Perhaps you don't say it in so many words, but you are letting everyone know that faith in Jesus Christ is better than anything this world has to offer.

Since this is true, don't be surprised when you are hated and persecuted. Remember, the Lord Jesus received treatment far worse than you'll ever be called upon to endure. Be assured that He will be with you, and that He will give you strength for every trial. Thousands have given their lives for Christ's sake, even during the last few years. The atheistic forces that took over their countries hated them, and many were put to death, but these believers endured persecution with courage and in triumph. They knew they belonged to God, and had relinquished claim to their own lives. They were willing to die if necessary, for they had already submitted to the "law of the cross." They were confident that a richer and fuller life awaited them in Glory.

If you have really acknowledged that you belong to God, and if you have truly died to yourself, you will be able to accept reviling words without retaliation, to endure hatred without bitter response, and to be misunderstood without whining in self-pity. In fact, you will show love to those who hate you. You will then be obeying the command Jesus gave His disciples, for He told them that when the world hated them, they were to bear witness (John 15:27). The person who has died to selfishness will give testimony to Christ's love. Our enemies are headed for eternal ruin, and we have the only message that can help them. We cannot, we must not, we dare not allow any self-concern to silence our lips. The Lord Jesus loved us when we were His enemies, and we must show the same attitude toward those who misuse us. When we do this, we will discover the secret of true happiness through adversity.

The apostles set an example for us to follow. They were beaten and imprisoned for preaching the Gospel before being released under solemn command never again to proclaim the name of Jesus. Did these humble men cringe in fear? Indeed not! Luke tells us that after their scourging they "departed from the presence of the council, rejoicing that they were counted worthy to suffer shame for his name" (Acts 5:41). They went out and preached again. Christian friend, if you will accept the "law of the cross'" as the principle for your life, you too will look upon affliction as an honor, and you will rejoice that through it you can glorify Jesus Christ.

II. Obedient Activity

The person who submits to the way of the cross as the pattern for fruitfulness and joy, even in adverse circumstances, will also engage in strenuous spiritual activity. You will never be victorious over suffering while you have self on the throne of your life. If you really want all your greed and pride to be destroyed, you must have a deep longing for holiness, a genuine prayer interest in others, and an earnest desire to serve the Lord in whatever way you can; not for your praise but for His glory.

A vital ingredient in the life of a radiant Christian is a longing for Christlikeness. If you really love Him the way you should, and if you truly hate sin, you will yearn to be like Jesus and to do His will. But when you think only in terms of selfish desires, you cannot endure trials in a victorious manner. Therefore, make likeness to Jesus Christ the aim and goal of your life. You will then transcend the difficulties and trials you must endure. The apostle Paul surrendered to the "law of the cross," and lived in great triumph. Read his epistles and you will find scores of references to rejoicing. Why? Because the moment he met the Lord Jesus he said, "Lord, what wilt thou have me to do?" (Acts 9:6). From that point on, the passion of this man's life was to know Christ better, to grow in conformity to Him, and to make Him known to others. He never forgot that he had been bought with a price, and that he now belonged to Jesus.

Do you exalt the Lord in your thinking? How earnestly do you desire to be like Him? Christian friend, the extent to which Christ has occupied the throne of your heart is the measure of your ability to overcome suffering in a triumphant manner. This involves saying "No" to yourself again and again, which is obeying our Lord's rule for discipleship, "If any man will come after me, let him deny himself, and take up his cross, and follow me" (Matthew 16:24). When growth in holiness and fellowship with Jesus Christ is more precious than earthly pleasures or joys, you will have the key to happiness in the midst of trouble.

Another essential for a life that is regulated by the "law of the cross" is intercessory prayer. Remember, Jesus said that we are not to love our own lives, but that we should follow His example of self-giving. This means that our prayers are to be unselfish in nature, for we will be far more interested in exalting our Savior and helping others than in promoting our own comfort, advancement, or reputation. Thus we will follow the example of the Lord Jesus.

Though He faced a dreadful night of trial and scourging, and knew it would be followed by His crucifixion the next morning, Jesus pleaded for others in that beautiful prayer recorded in John 17. The apostle Paul emulated his Lord, for he repeatedly declared in his epistles how he prayed for the saints. He didn't spend time begging God to give him things for his own comfort and needs. Writing to the Christians in Rome he said, "For God is my witness, whom I serve with my spirit in the gospel of his Son, that without ceasing I make mention of you always in my prayers" (Romans 1:9). His imprisonments, scourgings, shipwrecks, and hardships were of far less concern to him than the welfare of Christ's people.

Recently I was told of an aged saint whose health is failing. Instead of complaining or praying only for herself, she spends her sleepless hours at night in earnest intercession. And the result? She glows with the joy of the Lord and her prayers are being answered. Wonderful spiritual changes have come into the lives of many since she began her prayer ministry. Her life is bearing fruit, and she is finding true happiness even in these last few months of her earthly life. Unselfish prayer enriches the life of the one who prays and helps others find victory as well.

The "law of the cross" also demands totally selfless service. Jesus declared that the one who loves his life by seeking personal ease and pleasure will lose it. Such a life will be utterly fruitless. He went on to say, "If any man serve me, let him follow me" (John 12:26). The one who gives himself to Christ's service with wholehearted devotion and loyalty will have no reason to rebel against the Lord or distrust Him.

Let me suggest three ways you can prove in your experience that the abundant life is through the death of self. First, read the gospels, and observe how completely Christ gave Himself for our salvation. You will see that His death opened the way to Heaven, and you will respond to His call for complete surrender. You will also be thrilled and encouraged as you read the Acts of the Apostles, for you will discover that pleasures of sin and the dictates of the flesh did not rule them. They said a deliberate "No" to the enticements of evil or self-gratification, and thousands were swept into the kingdom of God as a result.

Secondly, go to a Christian library or bookstore and obtain the biographies of great servants of God like William Booth, George Mueller, and Hudson Taylor. These men demonstrated the truth that the person who dies to self and is willing to lose his life for Christ's sake has found the pathway to genuine happiness and true effectiveness. Such lives are filled with joy and make an impact which continues for generations.

Thirdly, surrender yourself to Jesus Christ. Own Him as your Lord and Master. Acknowledge that you belong to Him. Reject every selfish thought that comes to your mind, and make holiness and knowing Christ the passion of your life. Pray for others, and serve the Lord with zeal and fearlessness. This is the way to be happy in spite of adversity.

18

REJOICING IN HOPE

A Christian can possess real joy even when he knows that the adverse circumstances in his life will not improve. He has the assurance that he is in the hands of God, can enjoy fellowship with Jesus Christ, and rests in the prospect of eternal glory. Many times humble believers, standing at the door of death, have actually brought comfort to grieving loved ones by telling of their own joyous anticipation of meeting the Lord Jesus face to face. While one who does not believe on Christ may be courageous, no humanly conceived religion or philosophy can give certainty and joy to dying people. Only the Gospel of Jesus Christ can offer these, for it alone proclaims a living Savior who destroyed the power of death through resurrection. Paul declares that those who have been justified through faith have "peace with God," and that they "rejoice in hope of the glory of God" (Romans 5:2). Yes, even in the face of death, the believer can rejoice, for he possesses a fourfold hope: the imminent return of Christ, a personal meeting with the Lord Jesus, a resurrection body, and a Heavenly home.

I. The Hope of Christ's Return

Every Christian, regardless of circumstances, should eagerly anticipate the return of Jesus Christ. The Lord told His disciples it was necessary for Him to leave, but that He would come back again. This promise was repeated by the two angels at Christ's ascension.

> And while they looked steadfastly toward heaven as he went up, behold, two men stood by them in white apparel;
> Who also said, Ye men of Galilee, why stand ye gazing up into heaven? This same Jesus, who is taken up

from you into heaven, shall so come in like manner as ye have seen him go into heaven (Acts 1:10, 11).

The expectation of the return of the Lord Jesus was real and vivid to the early Christians. Paul reminded the believers in Thessalonica that they had "turned to God from idols, to serve the living and true God, and to wait for his Son from heaven . . ." (1 Thessalonians 1:9, 10).

My father found tremendous help in his conviction that Jesus Christ could come at any moment. There were occasions when he was bitterly attacked by those who hated his message, who distorted the things he said, or who unjustly accused him. Through all of this difficulty he continued to believe that his daily activities might be interrupted by the return of the Lord Jesus. On Dad's desk stood the motto "Perhaps Today," and it expressed the deep conviction of his heart.

Christians today have more reason than any other generation of believers to expect Christ's coming. Conditions in the world strikingly parallel the prophecies of Scripture concerning the endtime. Israel today is a nation in the land of Palestine as predicted in Ezekiel 37. The world situation today is such that the Western confederacy of ten kingdoms described in Daniel 2 and 7 could immediately become a reality. The whole world is getting prepared for a great centralized government which will regulate every area of life — an exact blueprint for the coming of the Antichrist, the evil world ruler spoken of in Revelation 13. In addition, the degradation of mankind that we see today conforms perfectly to Paul's words in 2 Timothy 3:1-5.

Dear Christian, the pain you endure will be made easier if you believe that today the trumpet may sound, and that you will be caught up without dying to be with Christ. Your rest will be sweeter if every night you can close your eyes believing that you may open them in Glory. Yes, Jesus is coming again. It may be today!

II. The Hope of Immediate Glory

While you wait for the Lord's return, you should also rest upon the hope of immediate glory if you die. All Christians would rather be translated from earth to Heaven without dying, but you should not look upon death as something to dread. The Lord Jesus will be with you when you are called upon to go through "the valley of the shadow," and you will see His face immediately after your final heartbeat. During the time between death and resurrection you will enjoy a conscious existence in Heaven. The Lord Jesus promised to meet the dying thief in Paradise on the very day they both died: "Verily I say unto thee, Today shalt thou be with me in paradise" (Luke 23:43).

Paul by inspiration told us that the time between death and resurrection is one of joy and fellowship. He declared that for the Christian dying is "gain," and that "to depart and to be with Christ . . . is far better."

> For to me to live is Christ, and to die is gain.
>   But if I live in the flesh, this is the fruit of my labor, yet what I shall choose I know not.
>   For I am in a strait between two, having a desire to depart and to be with Christ, which is far better (Philippians 1:21-23).

The words "to depart and to be with Christ" in their Greek construction indicate that the two events take place simultaneously. The moment the believer dies he is "with Christ."

The Christian therefore can be happy even when he knows that his life on earth will soon end. He has the assurance that Jesus Christ might come to take him without dying, but he is also confident that even death itself is the gateway to Glory. An unsaved man facing death has many questions that he cannot answer, and has nothing substantial in which he can place his faith. He can only hope against hope that his future will be better than the present—and it's hard to die that way. He may try to put up a good front for the sake of people he loves, but he cannot "rejoice in hope of the glory of God." The true believer, however, has certainty that rests upon faith in Jesus Christ. When the apostle Paul faced execution, he could say, "I am now ready to be offered" (2 Timothy 4:6). From that time until the present, thousands upon thousands of believers in Christ have displayed a serenity in the presence of death that the world cannot explain. This deep peace, this soul-stirring joy can be found only through faith in the Lord Jesus. When you believe in His person and work, you need not fear death, and your closing days can be filled with joy.

II. The Hope of the Resurrection

The suffering or sorrowing Christian also finds great comfort in the assurance that he and his believing loved ones, together with the saints of all the ages, will spend eternity in glorified human bodies. Jesus, having risen from death and ascended into Heaven, will be the leader of a great company of resurrected people. Paul declared,

> But now is Christ risen from the dead and become the firstfruits of them that slept.
> For since by man came death, by man came also the resurrection of the dead (1 Corinthians 15:20, 21).

Christian friend, it's painful to watch that dear one of yours wasting away, his body becoming thin and emaciated. It isn't pleasant to contemplate the gradual weakening of your own body as you grow older. But when you have the assurance that God will give you a brand new, tangible resurrection body, you can observe suffering and grow older without becoming morbid or despairing. The Bible tells us several facts about our life after death that give us great assurance now.

First, our resurrection bodies will be actual and corporeal. The apostle John said that when Jesus comes again we shall be "like him; for we shall see him as he is" (1 John 3:2). Our Lord's resurrection body was real, for the group of women to whom He appeared after His resurrection "came and held him by the feet, and worshiped him" (Matthew 28:9). When He suddenly appeared to the assembled disciples on the day of resurrection, passing through the walls of the locked upper room where they had gathered, He made certain they understood He was not a mere ghost-like apparition. He said,

> . . . Why are ye troubled? And why do thoughts arise in your hearts?
> Behold my hands and my feet, that it is I myself; handle me, and see; for a spirit hath not flesh and bones, as ye see me have.
> And when he had thus spoken, he showed them his hands and his feet (Luke 24:38-40).

The Lord Jesus then ate a piece of broiled fish to assure them that His body was physical in nature. He was the same Jesus they had known before His crucifixion, and His resurrection body was real.

In the second place, the resurrection body will be incorruptible and glorious. In this world the beauty of youth soon fades and the strength of manhood wanes, but the resurrection body will possess an enduring loveliness and continuing beauty. Many people in this world have physical imperfections, some of them stemming from the time of birth, which make life difficult. But we can rejoice in Paul's declaration that the body "is sown in corruption; it is raised in incorruption. It is sown in dishonor; it is raised in glory" (1 Corinthians 15:42, 43). That new body will surpass the one we now possess, even as a beautiful plant exceeds the seed from which it springs. The Bible teaches that someday Jesus Christ will "change our lowly body, that it may be fashioned like his glorious body, according to the working by which he is able even to subdue all things unto himself" (Philippians 3:21).

Third, the resurrection body will be characterized by power; that is, by strength and vitality. Paul affirms, "It is sown in weakness; it is raised in power" (1 Corinthians 15:43). Many people who take pride in their physical prowess are suddenly stricken by disease, crippled by an accident, or taken by death as the result of an aneurysm or heart attack. Every bedridden patient and every dead body in a casket preaches a powerful sermon on the subject of man's weakness. The resurrection body, however, will be strong and powerful. Reflect upon this whenever you are aware of your own declining strength, and thank God for the wonderful hope of resurrection.

Finally, the resurrection body will be spiritual and heavenly in nature. In this world man's inner being is contaminated by sin, and the body often becomes the instrument for the gratification of evil desires. The new body will be dominated by the redeemed spirit, which is sinless. Therefore Paul asserts, "It is sown a natural body; it is raised a spiritual body. There is a natural body, and there is a spiritual body" (1 Corinthians 15:44). The apostle is not talking about the physical material of our bodies, but is declaring that the resurrection body will be completely in tune with our redeemed spirit. It will be perfectly adapted for our new life in Heaven.

IV. THE HOPE OF HEAVEN

The Christian possesses another wonderful hope when death draws near — the prospect of a new home in Heaven. When a believer dies, he enters the place of which he is already a citizen, the heavenly Jerusalem. In the last two chapters of Revelation the apostle John sketches a picture of the city as it descends to rest upon the renewed earth.

> And I saw a new heaven and a new earth; for the first heaven and the first earth were passed away; and there was no more sea.
>
> And I, John, saw the holy city, new Jerusalem, coming down from God out of heaven, prepared as a bride adorned for her husband.
>
> And I heard a great voice out of heaven saying, Behold, the tabernacle of God is with men, and he will dwell with them, and they shall be his people, and God himself shall be with them, and be their God.
>
> And God shall wipe away all tears from their eyes; and there shall be no more death, neither sorrow, nor crying, neither shall there be any more pain; for the former things are passed away (Revelation 21:1-4).

In this place, beautiful beyond all description, every believer will have his own home, for Christ is there preparing a place for us (John 14:2).

In your Heavenly home you will never again shed tears. Here on earth you have wept, and you may carry thoughts and memories in your heart which often cause sadness, but before eternity begins God will wipe all tears from your eyes. The cuts and wounds and hurts of this life will be healed. In that new home death will be no more. In this world every family sooner or later experiences that awful feeling of emptiness — the dreadful vacuum caused by the death of a loved one. Truly, change and decay are all around us, but in our Heavenly home we will no longer live under the shadow of death. We will never again suffer the excruciating pain of cancer or arthritis, the discomfort following surgery, or the pounding punishment of a headache. Think of it, in our new home we will not even become weary, for a feeling of vigor and youthful energy will forever be ours.

In Heaven you will find no defiling substance, nor any person committing acts of desecration. Everything will be perfectly clean, and the moral defilement that marks earth today will not be present there. No wicked men or women will mar the purity of that eternal city to which you are going. God's Word declares,

> And there shall in no way enter into it anything that defileth, neither he that worketh abomination, or maketh a lie . . . (Revelation 21:27).

No violence! No rebellion! No lawlessness! No immorality! What a wonderful world!

Are you distressed as you think of your earthly life, your family circle broken by death, and your relationship marred by imperfections? Christian friend, God has a better place prepared for you. The tears, death, sorrow, crying, and pain of this present world will be gone forever. A home of infinite beauty and glory awaits you. Therefore, though you live in the midst of trouble, believe in God's promise of Heaven. Trust Him, for properly responding to the adversities of today will make the joys of your eternal tomorrow sweeter. By exercising your faith, you will indeed "rejoice in hope of the glory of God."

If you do not have this hope in Christ because you have not placed your trust in Him, bow your head and utter this simple prayer of faith: "Lord Jesus, I know I am a sinner who deserves Your wrath. I believe You died to pay for my sins, and that You are alive today. I am receiving You now as my Savior, my only hope of salvation. Amen."

> For whosoever shall call upon the name of the Lord shall be saved (Romans 10:13).

Part IV

HAPPINESS WITH

YOURSELF AND OTHERS

19

HOW TO LIVE WITH YOURSELF

Many people today find it difficult to live with themselves or with others. They experience so much inner tension, frustration, and fear, that they cannot be alone with their thoughts. Therefore they refuse to face the ultimate issues of life squarely and honestly, and throw themselves into the pursuit of pleasure, wealth, or fame. For the average individual, this may mean spending many hours in front of the television screen, reading sensual and erotic literature, or drinking to excess with companions who also are seeking to get away from themselves. An ever-increasing percentage of the young express their frustrations and fears through the use of hallucinating drugs, in violent demonstrations, and wild sexual orgies. Actually, the international discord, the racial strife, the divorce problem, and the suicide rate are reflections of man's inability to live with a philosophy of life that rules out God and considers man to be only an accident of nature—a meaningless blob. No one can live joyously, harmoniously, or helpfully unless he has peace within his own soul. You can't get along with others until you have an adequate view of yourself. You must be able to face life with all its tears, pain, and injustice, and still possess joy and hope.

The Bible tells us three things that are basic to an understanding of one's self. (1) You are a person who has been created in the image of God. (2) You are a sinner who needs divine forgiveness and a new nature. (3) God loves you and has provided the salvation you need.

I. You Are a Person

The declaration that you are a person may not seem significant to you, for it is something you have always assumed. Though you may have accepted the commonly held theory that man is only a highly developed animal, you have always recognized your ability to learn, to reason, to experience emotions, and to make intelligent choices. Perhaps you have no definite ideas about God, and you don't allow yourself to think a great deal about death and eternity. You're trying to make a go of things as they are, and you hope for the best. Now, this view of life may enable you to maintain a certain amount of mental composure and live on relatively good terms with your fellow men, but it will not give you deep inner peace. You will be without spiritual support when death invades your family circle or begins to blow hot on the back of your neck. You will have no hope. You need to find the Biblical answer to a very basic question — "Who am I?" The only alternative you have is the grim and hopeless position of unbelief.

The Bible states clearly and emphatically that God made man in His own image, distinct from the animal world.

> And God said, Let us make man in our image, after our likeness; and let them have dominion over the fish of the sea, and over the fowl of the air, and over the cattle, and over all the earth, and over every creeping thing that creepeth upon the earth.
>
> So God created man in his own image, in the image of God created he him; male and female created he them (Genesis 1:26, 27).

The Lord has endowed you and me with the elements of personality — a rational mind, genuine emotions, and a free will. True, we share some physical similarities to birds and beasts, but these likenesses are only superficial. Our ability to reason, to feel, and to make decisions sets us apart from all animals. Moreover, we are equipped to exercise dominion over the material world in which we live, and we possess a consciousness of God's existence, including an innate sense of right and wrong, and a realization of our responsibility to Him. Man's inner nature therefore confirms the Biblical teaching that we are not the products of a haphazard process of evolution, but that we are a special creation of God, made in His image, and destined for an eternity in either Heaven or Hell.

If you do not accept the Biblical teaching that man is the image-bearer of God, your only alternative is to believe you are an accident of nature, which logically demands that you deny the reality of your own personality. You see, an impersonal force operating through the evolutionary process could never produce a being who can really think, feel emotions, know right from wrong, and make intelligent decisions. Many non-Christian intellectuals acknowledge this, and therefore teach that man is completely under the control of chemical processes within his body or of psychological factors to which he has been subjected. These men declare, for example, that a person's feeling of love for his children may seem to be real and voluntary, but that it is nothing more than a programmed response like that of a computer. This would mean that the man who is true to his wife and works hard to provide for his family has not chosen to be this kind of person, and that the individual serving time in prison after a long series of crimes is in no way responsible for his conduct. By this theory, all of man's actions are classified as being automatic responses to data entering his computer-like brain, not the result of a genuine decision freely and rationally made. If this be true, the words "love," "hope," "joy," and "immortality" play a joke on humans, for they come to mind, but in actuality are meaningless concepts which have no reality.

The person who rejects God's Word must also see life as having no goal or meaning. The naturalist predicts eventual oblivion, for he says that the universe will someday run its course and become a chaotic mass of darkness and lifelessness. Sartre, one of the most eloquent proponents of an atheistic philosophy of life, admitted that not many people are able to live successfully without hope. But, let me remind you, you have only two alternatives from which you must chose. You are either a *person* created by God in His image, or you are a meaningless blob, an insignificant accident of nature without purpose or aim.

What you believe about yourself will also profoundly influence your day-by-day life upon earth. If you become a Christian, you will set your goals with eternal values in view, you will try to do God's will by loving Him and your fellow men, and you will rejoice in the prospect of a glorious eternity. On the other hand, if you accept the verdict of unbelief, you will set up temporary goals in an effort to fill the emptiness of your life. Since everyone is basically selfish, and each person strives for the same things, you will be involved in competition with others. Envy and frustration always grip the less successful, and soon folks are at each other's throats. James declares that this is the reason people quarrel and fight with one another the way they do.

> From where come wars and fightings among you? Come they not here, even of your lusts that war in your members?
> Ye lust, and have not; ye kill, and desire to have, and cannot obtain; ye fight and war, yet ye have not, because ye ask not (James 4:1, 2).

You must choose Christ or blind unbelief. Your decision will determine how effectively you will be able to live with yourself and others. Only if you believe God's Word will you be able to have a logical explanation of life as it is, and a transforming hope to give you a song in the darkest night.

II. You Are a Sinner

In addition to recognizing yourself as a person, you must also accept the Biblical teaching that you are a sinner. The first three chapters of Genesis tell us that man, created sinless and in God's image, chose to disobey God and go his own way. Mankind is now in rebellion against the Lord, and every aspect of the human personality has been tainted by sin. The apostle Paul declared,

> For they that are after the flesh do mind the things of the flesh; but they that are after the Spirit, the things of the Spirit.
> For to be carnally minded is death, but to be spiritually minded is life and peace.
> Because the carnal mind is enmity against God; for it is not subject to the law of God, neither, indeed, can be.
> So, then, they that are in the flesh cannot please God (Romans 8:5-8).

In other words, man in his own strength is not able to change his sinful nature or live in a manner pleasing to God.

The Biblical teaching that man is depraved is the only satisfactory explanation of the sad state of affairs in the world today. With every new generation the young confidently affirm that they can devise ways to bring in a world without war, injustice, or poverty, but these dreams are always shattered through human greed and wickedness. As a result, realistic thinkers no longer paint an optimistic picture when asked what the world will be like thirty years from now. In fact, many scientists are gloomily predicting great ecological disaster or nuclear war as inevitable. While brilliant minds have brought about amazing scientific and technological feats, human nature is just as cruel and selfish as ever, and man cannot be trusted with the power he has. Moreover, the senseless murders, gross sex crimes, violent riots, and war brutalities that make headlines, testify to the truth of the Biblical teaching that man is a sinner. If he were an evolving creature with no tendencies toward evil, he would not continue to do things which threaten to bring about his own destruction. His innate sense of self-preservation would deter him from such evils. Only if you believe the Biblical doctrine of sin can you understand why people behave the way they do.

This is also a practical truth, for a frustrated person cannot take the proper steps to remedy his condition until he knows what is wrong with himself. If you are to be delivered from the inner turmoil that is ruining your life, you must first accept the Biblical diagnosis that you are a sinner. If you assume that you are an accident of nature, you will prescribe the wrong cure for your malady. Human wisdom today is no better equipped to solve your deepest problems than it was when Paul wrote that "the wisdom of this world is foolishness with God" (1 Corinthians 3:19). Acknowledge that you are a sinner, and you will have taken a giant step toward deliverance. Remember, the Lord Jesus said that the Son of man came "not to call the righteous, but sinners to repentance."

III. You Are an Object of God's Love

Having come to the realization that you and your fellow men have been created in God's image but are fallen through sin, you are now ready to believe that you are an object of God's redeeming love. Yes, God loves sinners!

The Lord has proven His love for men. Many people despair of a God who loves man, because they see life filled with suffering, heartbreak, and injustice; but God proved His love when He sent His eternal Son into the world to die for our sins. Every Sunday school child has memorized the verse which declares,

> For God so loved the world, that he gave his only begotten Son, that whosoever believeth in him should not perish, but have everlasting life (John 3:16).

The apostle Paul wrote,

> For when we were yet without strength, in due time Christ died for the ungodly.
> For scarcely for a righteous man will one die; yet perhaps for a good man some would even dare to die.
> But God commendeth his love toward us in that, while we were yet sinners, Christ died for us (Romans 5:6-8).

Yes, God loves you. He places great value upon you, even though you are sinful, and though you grieve Him by the way you think, talk, and act. If He didn't love you, the Lord Jesus would never have become a member of the human race to die the horrible death on the cross for your sins.

It isn't easy to understand how a loving God can allow life to be so full of suffering and heartbreak. But you must recognize that He is not only loving but also holy. His inherent righteousness makes it necessary for Him to demand right conduct from His moral creatures. When we do wickedly, His justice requires that our sins be punished. Man's sinfulness is therefore the reason for all the pain and tears that mar human life today, and no one should blame God for these things. Moreover, the Lord is absolutely just, and someday He will rectify every wrong and punish every sin. But, "God is love" (1 John 4:8), He delights in mercy, and His heart today yearns for sinners even as it did when He said,

> . . . As I live, saith the Lord God, I have no pleasure in the death of the wicked, but that the wicked turn from his way and live; turn ye, turn from your evil ways; for why will ye die . . . ? (Ezekiel 33:11).

God's love devised the plan of salvation for sinners. The eternal Son, the second person of the Trinity, took upon Himself our humanity. He lived a perfect life for us, then went to the cross to take the punishment our sin deserves. He died for us, rose from the grave to break death's power, and today offers salvation to all who will believe on Him.

God's love for you is not just a theory to discuss, but a glorious truth you can experience. Tell the Lord Jesus that you believe on Him, and that you are receiving Him today. The Bible declares, "But as many as received him, to them gave he power to become the children of God, even to them that believe on his name" (John 1:12).

What a difference between the person who believes the verdict of atheistic evolution and the one who accepts Jesus Christ! The unbeliever finds it difficult to live with himself, for he doesn't really know who he is, cannot tell why he is here, and has no hope for the future. He is in constant inner turmoil. While his heart tells him that he is a sinner accountable to God, he keeps trying to convince himself that this is not true. He yearns wistfully for a better world beyond the grave, even while his naturalistic philosophy tells him that death ends all. He may be able to compose himself and show raw courage, as did Bertrand Russell shortly before his death when he said, "I've had my good innings." But such a person will never find true joy or be able to bring comfort, strength, and cheer to a bereaved or dying person.

The Christian, on the other hand, has found inner peace. He knows he should be a better person than he is, and often wishes he were, but he finds joy in his fellowship with the Lord and is comforted in the realization that his sins have been forgiven. He is conscious of his weakness and inadequacy, but rejoices that he is a child of God destined for a glorious eternity in Heaven. These assurances enable the believer to live with the thoughts that come to him during the night, and to get along with his fellow men.

He can also be an inspiration to those with whom he comes in contact. A Christian periodical recently featured the story of a girl who was blinded and paralyzed as a result of spinal meningitis which struck her almost immediately after graduating from high school. She today radiates the joy of the Lord, and carries out a ministry of service and blessing to many others. No person without God and hope could possibly duplicate what this girl is doing.

Are you able to live with yourself? Can you, when you are all alone, reflect upon life's meaning and the fact that you will die someday? What would *you* do if tomorrow you suddenly were blinded or paralyzed? Would you bitterly curse your bad luck or be hard to live with? Or would you look to the Lord in faith, believing even this to be part of His loving purpose for your life? The pathway of unbelief is that of frustration, bitterness, and, at very best, stoical endurance. The way of faith is that of trust, confidence, and hope. If you know Christ, you will find joy and strength to live with yourself, to be at peace with others, and to be an uplifting influence in the lives of your fellow men.

20

THE HUSBAND AND WIFE

Someone has said that the three stages of modern family life are matrimony, acrimony, and alimony. This is indeed a sad commentary upon many of today's homes. A large percentage of marriages are broken by divorce, and some people unblushingly break their marital vows but keep the family unit intact only because it is less complicated than a legal dissolution would be. Furthermore, the voices of those who advocate free love are sounding out their call for the abandonment of the family structure. They baldly predict that the next generation will no longer be under the tyranny of this concept they consider primitive and outmoded.

The denial of the divinely ordered nature of the family is nothing new. In the Greco-Roman world of the first century A.D., men regarded their wives as mere property like a slave or an animal. They divorced their mates capriciously and demanded total fidelity from their wives, while they engaged in immoral relations with prostitutes or with homosexuals. The Gospel of Jesus Christ came upon this scene with the revolutionary teaching that men and women are spiritual equals, and that marriage is a sacred lifelong union, demanding sexual fidelity on the part of both the husband and wife.

The tension, strife, and unhappiness that is breaking up homes today is a direct result of a general departure from God and His Word. The Bible sets forth specific instruction for both husbands and wives; and when its admonitions are heeded, each member of the family can find love, comfort, strength, and joy in the home. A husband and wife who wish to live together harmoniously should take to heart the Biblical teaching regarding (1) the nature of marriage, and (2) the mutual obligations of each toward the other.

I. The Nature of Marriage

The Bible teaches that marriage is the most intimate of all human ties, and that this relationship is both exclusive and enduring.

Marriage is an exclusive relationship. The creation story as recorded in Genesis 1 and 2 clearly establishes the truth that God intended one woman and one man to be united, and that no other person can share this union. After God had fashioned Eve from one of Adam's ribs and presented her to him, the man very movingly declared, "This is now bone of my bones, and flesh of my flesh; she shall be called Woman, because she was taken out of Man" (Genesis 2:23), and Moses by inspiration added, "Therefore shall a man leave his father and his mother, and shall cleave unto his wife; and they shall be one flesh" (Genesis 2:24). The husband and wife are to be physically, emotionally, and spiritually *one*, and whenever either of the parties in the marriage contract loses sight of the "one flesh" nature of marriage and engages in sexual relations with another person, the husband-wife relationship is scarred. Furthermore, when a society departs from God's standard to the practice of polygamy, or thinks lightly of sexual infidelity, the consequences are disastrous. Good homes are the indispensable foundation stones for a materially prosperous and morally healthy nation.

Husbands and wives must be convinced of the exclusiveness of the marriage relationship, for then they will work out their problems, forgive each other's faults, and help one another to make the marriage a success. Then, too, sexual union within the bounds of wedlock not only enriches the lives of both, but also enhances their realization of total oneness. On the other hand, when the sacredness of marriage is denied, a vital incentive for harmony is lost; and those who engage in the sexual act outside of marriage, by selfishly exploiting another person for temporary and superficial pleasure, lose their capacity to love unselfishly. Therefore, a high view of the sacredness and exclusiveness of marriage must be emphasized today.

Marriage is for life. That God intends marriage to endure for the lifetime of the two partners is clear from the words of Christ, ". . . What, therefore, God hath joined together, let not man put asunder" (Matthew 19:6). Homes are filled with strife and contention when neither party in the marriage makes a sincere effort to understand the other, and if the thought that a divorce and new marriage may be the solution is entertained. If every husband and wife considered marriage a sacred and lifelong relationship to be broken only by death, many homes would be far different than they are.

II. MUTUAL OBLIGATION OF HUSBAND AND WIFE

In order that a loving and satisfying relationship may exist between husband and wife, both parties must also obey the Scriptures which set forth their mutual responsibility toward one another. No institution can run smoothly and efficiently unless the people involved have a clear understanding of their authority, their duties, and their privileges — and this is certainly true of the home. Since both Paul and Peter give specific instructions to married couples and address the wives first, this is the order we will follow in our study. The Bible exhorts the woman to take the place of *loving submission,* and to live a life marked by *genuine spirituality.*

Paul commanded women to be in submission to their husbands when he wrote, "Wives, submit yourselves unto your own husbands, as unto the Lord" (Ephesians 5:22). And Peter expressed this same demand when he said, "In the same manner, ye wives, be in subjection to your own husband" (1 Peter 3:1). At first sight this requirement might seem to contradict the New Testament teaching that women are the spiritual equals of men. Since it is true that "there is neither Jew nor Greek, there is neither bond nor free, there is neither male nor female; for ye are all one in Christ Jesus" (Galatians 3:28), why should the wife be in this place of subservience in the home? The answer lies in understanding that the wife's submission is not a reflection upon her value and dignity as a person. The Bible never denies her complete spiritual equality with her husband, nor does it in any way demean her personal worth or nobility. Instead, this subjection is one of function. Every organization needs a leader, every team must have a manager or head coach, and God has ordained that the husband take the place of leadership in the home. Even as a colonel's rank does not indicate that he has less personal worth than the general to whom he is responsible, so the wife's place of submission in no way indicates that God places less value upon her than her husband. Moreover, the submission of a Christian wife is not rendered out of a feeling of inferiority nor in the spirit of cringing fear. It issues from her love for God and her husband, and from her desire for order and harmony in the home.

In addition to a sweet attitude of submission, the believing wife must also possess genuine spirituality. Peter emphasized this when he said,

> In the same manner, ye wives, be in subjection to your own husband that, if any obey not the word, they also may without the word be won by the behavior of the wives,
> While they behold your chaste conduct coupled with fear;
> Whose adorning, let it not be that outward adorning of braiding the hair, and of wearing of gold, or of putting on of apparel,
> But let it be the hidden man of the heart in that which is not corruptible, even the ornament of a meek and quiet spirit, which is in the sight of God of great price (1 Peter 3:1-4).

While the apostle was addressing Christian wives whose husbands were still pagans, for he knew that such women needed special counsel and help, the admonitions are applicable to every believing wife today. If she is the kind of woman God wants her to be, she will manifest it by a true concern for her husband's eternal welfare and by her modesty and inward beauty.

A truly spiritual woman will possess a genuine concern for her husband's soul. Peter declared that the wife of an unsaved man is to be in subjection in order that her mate may become a Christian.

> In the same manner, ye wives, be in subjection to your own husbands that, if any obey not the word, they also may without the word be won by the behavior of the wives (I Peter 3:1).

A man may be antagonistic to the Word of God and be offended if his wife quotes Scripture to him, but such an individual might become a believer if his marriage partner displays a gracious and respectful spirit. Her sweetness and purity will expose him to the pricking of the arrow of conviction, accomplishing what her verbal testimony or sincere exhortations could not do. Such an attitude is not always easy. Some men are cruel to their wives, and their lives are so sin-blighted that it is difficult to have a feeling of respect for them. But if the believing spouse lives in fellowship with her Lord, God will give her grace and strength. Furthermore, someday she will be rewarded for her faithfulness.

The Christian wife of a believing husband should also possess a sincere longing for his spiritual good. She will seek to maintain an atmosphere which will be spiritually helpful to the husband. Many a man with a weak Christian testimony and a faltering faith has become a stalwart believer through the faithful prayers and uplifting influence of his devoted wife. Remember, two people who share a deep love for Christ will walk in harmony!

A truly spiritual woman will also be marked by her modesty and inward beauty. Peter said,

> Whose adorning, let it not be that outward adorning of braiding the hair, and of wearing of gold, or of putting on of apparel,
> But let it be the hidden man of the heart in that which is not corruptible, even the ornament of a meek and quiet spirit, which is in the sight of God of great price (1 Peter 3:3, 4).

What the apostle here requires is an attractive self-restraint, a proper sense of what is really important. A wife makes a serious mistake if she thinks that the latest styles in hairdress and garments to enhance her physical attractiveness are of prime importance, and many a marriage in which no expense has been spared to produce the finest in clothing and jewelry has ended in divorce. Of course, the physical aspect of marriage is important, and every woman should be careful about her personal cleanliness and appearance, taking seriously her conjugal responsibilities. A spiritual woman will not give herself to luxurious and senseless extravagance, but instead will manifest a love for God and a proper respect for her husband, her life being marked by unselfishness, purity, kindness, and serenity.

In addition, a Christian woman must remain with her

unsaved mate and do her best to make the marriage a success as long as he wishes, and as long as he is faithful to her.

> And the woman who hath an husband that believeth not, and if he be pleased to dwell with her, let her not leave him (1 Corinthians 7:13).

She is to submit to him if it does not involve a conflict with her higher loyalty to Christ, and she should seek to win her mate to the Lord.

In summary, the believing wife will try to do her part to make the home as Christian as it possibly can be. To the extent that it is effective and helpful, she will speak to her husband about the things of God, encouraging him, and earnestly entreating him. But most of all she will seek that true loveliness' which is the result of continuous fellowship with the Lord Jesus. This more than anything else will promote the spiritual welfare of her husband and bring about harmony in the home.

The Christian husband also has a solemn responsibility toward his wife, and Paul expressed it in one brief sentence: "Husbands, love your wives, even as Christ also loved the church, and gave himself for it" (Ephesians 5:25). The love the husband is to show his wife must be marked by the same self-sacrificial devotion the Lord Jesus manifested toward the Church when He gave His life on the cross. True, the woman is also commanded to love her husband (Titus 2:4), but God places a stronger demand for complete selflessness upon the man. The husband's role as the head of the home is a privilege, but it is also a great responsibility, for he must renounce all selfishness and always seek the best for his wife, even dying for her if necessary.

This obligation of the man to love his wife as Christ loved the Church also involves the elements of consideration, protection, and support. Peter declared,

> In like manner, ye husbands, dwell with them according to knowledge, giving honor unto the wife, as unto the weaker vessel, and as being heirs together of the grace of life, that your prayers be not hindered (1 Peter 3:7).

As the husband lives with his wife, he should recognize that her womanhood entails some special physical and psychological problems which he doesn't encounter. It is only in this sense that the woman is "the weaker vessel." The husband must therefore honor his wife as his spiritual equal, and take the leadership in the home that he might better strengthen, support, and protect her. He must never use his authority in a boorish or overbearing manner to dominate her, but is to be kind, tender, and protective.

The husband's Christlike love for his wife also demands that he bear in mind that he and his wife as spiritual equals are "heirs together of the grace of life" (1 Peter 3:7). He must therefore create a spirit of mutuality in which his wife as a woman and he as a man share the joys and sorrows, the delights and disappointments, the laughter and tears of human existence.

When a man really seeks always to promote his mate's welfare, is considerate, tender, and kind, and shares all of life with her, they will have an effective prayer life together. Peter declares that obedience to the exhortations of Scripture is important, "that your prayers be not hindered" (1 Peter 3:7). Believing husbands and wives should pray together regularly, and, if they do, they will keep their relationship free from strife and bitterness. Any kind of friction experienced by a believing couple will make effective mutual prayer impossible. Therefore, problems must be settled daily before they result in deep wounds or bitter attitudes.

In closing, let me ask you wives, "Are you fulfilling the Biblical demand to be a submissive and truly godly woman in the home? Through your prayers and conduct, are you trying hard to be a spiritual help to your husband?" And you husbands, "Do you love your wife as Christ loved the Church? Do you seek always to help her, to be kind, tender, and considerate to her?" If either or both of you have failed, take up the Bible and read Ephesians 5:22-33 and 1 Peter 3:1-7. Then drop to your knees together, confess your failings, and ask God to help you. Learn to love each other and enrich your partner's life. The Lord stands ready to assist you if you will honestly seek to follow His admonition and if you earnestly look to Him for help.

21

PARENTS AND CHILDREN

A certain amount of mutual distrust and misunderstanding has always existed between the generations, but the tension has never been so pronounced as it is today. Many concerned people have proposed solutions to the problem. Some contend that the need is for better communication between parents and children, and most of us will acknowledge that this would help. But this does not get to the heart of the problem, which is spiritual in nature. Most adults have completely ignored God, or, if they profess faith, they conduct themselves in a manner inconsistent with the belief they claim to possess. As a result, their children have grown up in either a totally godless atmosphere or have been sickened by the hypocrisy of the older generation.

Some sincere youth are disturbed by the greed they see around them, the way people exploit one another and pollute the earth's air and water with no regard for public welfare. They do not hate their parents nor those who are in authority, but with youthful idealism they attack present injustices and propose sweeping changes. When these young people try to talk to older folk, they encounter defensive attitudes, and they are frustrated by the unwillingness of adults to acknowledge the mistakes of the past. Such youth need the help and encouragement of their elders who also possess compassion and concern.

Sad to say, all of the young are not sincerely trying to do what is right. Many sons and daughters are breaking the hearts of their parents by their conduct. They show no respect, but ridicule those in authority and live without moral restraint. With only a superficial understanding of the issues, and with a naive confidence in their ability to solve the world's problems, they whip themselves into a frenzy of hatred for the establishment and openly flout the laws of God and man. A large percentage are destroying themselves through the use of drugs and by engagement in every form of gross immorality.

The tragic clash between youth and adults, along with the growing breakdown of morality, will never be solved by mere dialogue and better communication. Nothing short of a Bible-based faith and commitment to the Lord Jesus will cure the greed and meet the deep spiritual need of both generations. Therefore we must turn to the Bible, and heed its message regarding the mutual responsibilities of parents and children.

I. THE OBLIGATIONS OF CHILDREN TO PARENTS

The Bible clearly demands that sons and daughters render both obedience and honor to their parents.

The first duty of a Christian son or daughter to parents is obedience, a submission which flows from reverence for the Lord Jesus as well as from love and gratitude to the mother and father. Paul says, "Children, obey your parents in the Lord; for this is right" (Ephesians 6:1). A child who has received Christ will obey his parents because he knows this is pleasing to the Lord. Parental authority will be recognized and exercised in a Christian home, for this is God's order. Obedience in the home is a foundational requirement for a harmonious society. When young people do not respect or obey their parents, they manifest the same attitude outside the home. Leaders in government and education face grave problems with the youth who have not learned the meaning of the word "obedience." Juvenile delinquency, drug abuse, sexual promiscuity, and general lawlessness are evident by the time children reach junior high school. Society is paying a heavy price for its departure from the Scriptures, and the only solution is a return to the Biblical concept of the family. When children love the Lord, they will obey their parents and be good citizens.

In addition to obedience, the Lord requires that Christian sons and daughters honor their parents.

> Honor thy father and mother (which is the first commandment with promise),
>   That it may be well with thee, and thou mayest live long on the earth (Ephesians 6:2, 3).

Honor is closely related to obedience, but they are not identical. A child should obey his parents even if he thinks their requirements are unfair. The obligation is not absolute, however, for a Christian child might find it necessary to disobey a parent's demand that he lie, steal, or in some other way break God's law. Furthermore, every young person reaches the age at which he must begin to make his own decisions. A son need not enter an occupation he detests just because his parents have chosen it for him. Nor have the father and mother the right to dictate his choice of a mate. The obligation of obedience is therefore not always mandatory, but the requirement of honor is unqualified. A son or daughter must show respect and honor to parents even if they are completely undeserving, and this responsibility lasts throughout life.

One of the great tragedies of our day is the fact that many fine parents are practically ignored by their offspring. Aged people are often lonely and forsaken because the children they have raised seem to have no time for them. Every believer has an obligation to visit his parents regularly if possible, or if they are separated by many miles, to write or telephone them frequently. An elderly person, whether living alone or in a rest home with others, will be a happier and more agreeable person if sons and daughters fulfill their God-ordained responsibility.

If a parent is unsaved and lives an evil life, it may not be easy to show him honor, but this is still God's demand. As long as such a parent lives, his sons or daughters must remember him in prayer, speak respectfully of him, and treat him as kindly as possible, no matter how unworthy he may be.

The apostle Paul declared that those who honor their parents have a special promise from God, "That it may be well with thee, and thou mayest live long on the earth" (Ephesians 6:3). When God gave Israel the law, He assured children who obeyed their parents that they would live a long life in the land of Palestine (Deuteronomy 5: 16), and the apostle by inspiration applied the essence of this promise to believers in the Church. This does not mean that honoring parents is a magical formula for a long and happy life, but it indicates a general principle. Even apart from God's special providence, an obedient child who honors his parents has a far greater likelihood to live long and happily than the one who is rebellious. A disobedient child is likely to become an undisciplined person, and this in turn may lead him into vice, drug abuse, or dissipation.

Furthermore, the son or daughter who obeys and honors parents because of love for the Lord will experience the promise, "that it may be well with thee." Such a person will possess inner peace, will love his fellow men, and will know the joy of deliverance from the tyranny of greed and sensualism. The undisciplined person, on the other hand, has no peace, is a slave of sin, and has lost the ability to love unselfishly. Therefore, whenever children who love the Lord obey and honor their parents, society will be greatly benefited, for they will be the kind of people who promote harmony and good feeling in every area of life.

II. THE DUTY OF PARENTS TO CHILDREN

The Bible also sets forth the duties of a father and mother to their children. When parents observe these inspired exhortations, they will very likely find their children a source of joy and satisfaction. Many fathers and mother who sense a wide rift between themselves and their offspring are largely responsible for this condition, for they have never fulfilled the parental role in accordance with these Biblical directives. In Ephesians 6, Paul addresses fathers (but certainly what he says also applies to mothers):

> And, ye fathers, provoke not your children to wrath, but bring them up in the nurture and admonition of the Lord (Ephesians 6:4).

This verse contains two distinct admonitions, one negative and the other positive: (1) do not provoke your children to wrath, and (2) bring them up in the nurture and admonition of the Lord.

The words, "do not provoke your children to wrath," are quite similar to the thought Paul expressed in Colossians 3:21 when he said, "Father, provoke not your children to anger, lest they be discouraged." The idea is that parents must not exasperate their children and thus embitter them.

The first thing the parent must guard against is inconsistency. To make severe demands of a child while not strictly regulating one's own life causes the young person to feel wronged and leads to frustration. If the parent punishes a child for lying, when the youngster knows that his folks sometimes use deceit to further their own ends, he invites rebellion and distrust. Even small children are perceptive enough to see the inconsistency of parents who indulge in tobacco, alcohol, and in overeating, while refusing sweets to them on the ground that such food is not healthful. And they may soon express their inner rebellion and frustration by secretly smoking, drinking, or worse still, using hallucinating drugs. Every parent must examine his own life, and evaluate the demands he places upon his children. He must avoid all inconsistency and hypocrisy.

Adults must also resist the tendency to speak condescendingly to the young, giving the impression that they have nothing worthwhile to contribute. A parent who always gives advice, continually plays the part of an expert, and never acknowledges that the young person has a good idea, will do untold damage to that budding young life. He needs the opportunity to express himself, and those who listen will find that much of what he says has real value. True, some declarations of the young may seem somewhat shocking, but a Christian parent should be able to calmly and effectively discuss these assertions in the light of the Bible. Every father and mother should keep the door of communication open and be willing to accept some new idea. Certain truths are eternal and unchanging, but some of yesterday's answers do not solve today's problems. A frank discussion of the enduring principles found in the Bible, and of their relationship to the present, will be helpful to both the youth and adults, and will result in mutual understanding and respect.

Furthermore, parents must practice restraint when they are inclined to be overprotective. Children should be shielded from some of life's hard blows. They should be warned against dangers, but a child must not be forbidden to engage in the normal activities of others his own age simply because a risk of injury is involved. Such a young person will never gain self-confidence, will feel inferior to others, and will finally resent his parents when he realizes what they have done. Every parent must recognize that some hazards are inevitable in life, and must exercise faith in God's providential care of His children.

Parents are also cautioned to keep from undue harshness or brutality. Some men easily become angry and use their superior strength to inflict severe punishment. A parent must also shun the use of sarcasm and other devices which crush the child and make him wonder if he is really loved.

In summary, every parent must be careful that his actions do not provoke the child to bitterness, frustration, or humiliation. The young person must sense that his parents care for him, that they consider his conversation worthwhile and interesting. A son or daughter should be able to discuss his problems and viewpoints with his parents freely, and with the confidence that they will listen attentively and react rationally. Christian fathers and mothers will do well to take seriously the injunction, "provoke not your children to wrath'" (Ephesians 6:4).

The positive aspect of the parents' duty to their children is expressed in the words, "but bring them up in the nurture and admonition of the Lord." The Greek words translated "bring them up" present a picture of tender care — a direct contrast to the kind of treatment that would provoke a child to anger or plunge him into discouragement. Gentleness in parental dealing cannot be overemphasized. Baby chicks may be hatched by the thousands in incubators and seem to do well without a mother or father, but God made human beings with a very basic need for love. In today's busy world, many parents never take opportunity to show tender concern for their children's welfare, and many young people grow up feeling that no one cares for them, and this in turn leads some of them into undesirable conduct.

Care involves *discipline,* for the word "nurture" in Ephesians 6:4 carries the thought of chastening. It refers to the setting of rules and regulations, the promise of rewards, and the warning of penalties — all of which are necessary in the proper rearing of a child. Firmness and punishment are essential, and they are effective, but they will only be helpful when administered in love.

Proper care also includes *instruction,* which is the meaning of the word rendered "admonition" in Ephesians 6:4. A parent who is too busy to talk to his growing children, instructing them in the things of God, is failing in a most vital responsibility with which God has charged him. Young people who are taught to love Christ both by word and example, and are then led into a thorough understanding of the Scriptures, will be well-equipped to meet life's temptations and trials. They will love their parents, be good to their fellow men, and live in obedience to the laws of God. (See Proverbs 22:6.)

In conclusion, the relationship between youth and adults need not be marred by misunderstanding and mutual distrust. The two generations should enjoy one another, and both the young and their elders should be able to share a rich and rewarding life that glorifies the Lord. Children must give heed to the Scriptures, love the Lord Jesus Christ, and show their parents obedience and honor. Adults are to live godly lives, instruct their children in the fear of the Lord, avoid inconsistency, keep the door of communication open, and manifest a tender concern for the young. This is the pathway that will bring harmony to the home and will produce the kind of citizens that will enrich the community.

22

LIVING IN SOCIETY

In discussing the subject, "How to Live With Yourself and Others," we first pointed out that everyone must have an adequate view of himself before he can experience a friendly and delightful relationship with others. He must reject the idea that he is a mere animal, an accidental product of blind evolution, and believe the Biblical picture of himself as a person created in God's image, fallen through sin, but the object of the Lord's redeeming love. We then considered the basic unit of society — the family — and presented the Biblical teaching regarding the duties of husbands and wives to one another, and set forth the mutual responsibilities of parents and their children. If the homes of a country are ruled by Christ, and are marked by obedience, respect, love and tenderness, the whole of society will reap great benefits.

In this chapter we will consider the Christian as he lives in society. He daily encounters people who disappoint him. He must associate with evil people who lie, steal, cheat, live immorally, and use vile language. He also contacts some who hate him because he is a believer, and do all they can to hurt him. How is a child of God to get along in a world made up of erring, sinful, and hate-filled people? The Bible answers this question, setting forth standards by which a believer in Christ is to regulate his life in society, and it is to these principles that we will direct our attention.

I. Living With Fallen Humanity

The first problem is that of getting along with relatives, friends, and acquaintances. These people may be outstanding citizens and loyal church members, but some of them have personality traits you can't stand, and others have disappointed you or have made it clear that they don't like you. Now let me declare unequivocally that if you are a Christian, you have absolutely no right to despise people who rankle you. Neither should you throw up your hands in dismay when you are disappointed in someone for whom you held a high regard. Nor should you become hateful toward one who has wronged you or doesn't like you. If you have received Jesus Christ as your Savior, you are under a solemn obligation to obey His injunction, "A new commandment I give unto you, that ye love one another; as I have loved you, that ye also love one another" (John 13:34).

Reflect upon what our Lord said, "Love . . . as I have loved you!" Apply these words to your spiteful attitude toward certain people, and to your treatment of some folks who grate on your nerves. How about the way you avoid people because you feel superior to them? Don't you think the Lord sees some unlovely things in you? Yet He continues to love you! Wouldn't you be ashamed if your loved ones and dearest friends knew some of your secret thoughts as Christ does? Yet He doesn't shun you or refuse to be your Companion! Remember that we are all members of the one human family, and we are a fallen race. God graciously forgives us, and He continues to deal with us as His children in spite of all our failures. He knows that we are weak, erring, and prone to sin even after we have received His salvation. The Psalmist declared,

> As a father pitieth his children, so the Lord pitieth them that fear him.
> For he knoweth our frame; he remembereth that we are dust (Psalm 103:13, 14).

One of the serious faults of people in our churches today is their reluctance to befriend those who are not naturally attractive and likable. We tend to develop cliques, and some for whom Christ died and with whom He fellowships are shut out of our lives. What if the Lord Jesus dealt with us the way we treat others? Realizing that we ourselves are far from perfect, let us overlook the faults of others. Let us overcome our natural aversion to some folks, and love them as Christ loves us. Remember that we are alike members of the fallen race, each needing forgiveness and help.

The apostle Paul gave us an exhortation we ought to take to heart: "And be ye kind one to another, tenderhearted, forgiving one another, even as God, for Christ's sake, hath forgiven you" (Ephesians 4:32). This inspired admonition should be applied in the home, at church, in school, in the community, and at work or play. You will find that others' faults are no more serious than your own. In fact, some of the people you thought you could never like, will become dear friends and you will enjoy their company. Most of them will respond to love when you express it consistently, and if they are convinced of your sincerity.

II. Getting Along With Evil People

Believers must also learn to get along with people who are blasphemous, immoral, cruel, or completely unscrupulous. It may be necessary for us to live next door to such folks, or to spend hours with them daily at our places of employment. On the streets and in places of business one mingles with those who use gutter language or show no respect for God's name, and young people in secular colleges encounter many who delight in proclaiming their godlessness and demonstrating their wickedness.

What is the believer to do when confronted with blasphemy, vile language, or other evidences of an ungodly attitude? A strong rebuke or warning from his lips may invite derision and a new outburst of profanity or verbal filth. The Christian is therefore tempted to do nothing, but he must realize that Christ died for sinners, and that these wicked people are candidates for salvation. For this reason he must not ignore them, avoid them, nor look at them disdainfully with pharisaical pride. The fourth chapter of John tells us how compassionately Jesus treated the immoral woman He met at the well, and in the seventh chapter of this same gospel we read His words of forgiveness and assurance to one who had been taken in adultery. He gave His salvation to a criminal who hung on a cross alongside His own, when that man looked to Him in a repentance and faith. Later He spoke from Heaven to Saul of Tarsus, a bitter enemy of the early Christians, forgave his sin, and transformed him into the greatest apostle of the early church. The Lord Jesus loved sinners, sought them out, and redeemed all who placed their faith in Him.

Christian friend, your heart attitude toward that wicked person will largely determine the degree of your effectiveness in helping him. If you despise him and have no feeling of compassion for him, you will be able to exert no influence upon him for good. If you consider yourself better than he, forgetting that you possess the same sinful nature he does, you will drive him deeper into his sin. You may guard your words and try in every way possible to hide your thoughts, but he will sense your attitude and be turned away from you and the faith you profess.

If you and I do not feel a burden of compassion for those who are lost, we ought to get down upon our knees before the Lord and confess our spiritual coldness. Christ commanded us, "Thou shalt love thy neighbor as thyself" (Matthew 19:19). If the sight of wicked people day by day moving closer to a Christless eternity does not grieve us, we are living in disobedience to the Lord Jesus. We should therefore confess our sin, and ask God to kindle a fire of love and compassion within us. Then, motivated by the love of Christ, we will give the most wicked person a genuine smile, which tells him that we love him. We will speak words to him that are kind and helpful. We will perform deeds that will confirm in his mind our sincere interest in his eternal welfare.

When a Christian possesses genuine concern and manifests sincere love for the wicked, one of two things will happen. They will either be drawn toward us and respond to the message of the Gospel, or they will become more hostile. Many people will believe the Good News and receive the Lord Jesus as Savior. Some may not become Christians, but will nevertheless express appreciation for our way of life, and will acknowledge that our faith is an uplifting influence in the community. True, as stated before, a few who are confirmed in evil will hate us more intensely than ever. They may even persecute us. The Lord Jesus warned His disciples of this when He said,

> If ye were of the world, the world would love its own; but because ye are not of the world, but I have chosen you out of the world, therefore the world hateth you.
> Remember the word that I said unto you, The servant is not greater than his Lord. If they have persecuted me, they will also persecute you . . . (John 15:19, 20).

We should not allow such hatred to deter us from the pathway of compassion, prayer, and love. We may be sure that the people who are helped by our testimony and consistent living will greatly outnumber those who are stirred up to deep resentment and bitter hostility. Even some of those who hate us may later turn to Jesus Christ.

III. Getting Along With Those Who Hate Us

When a Christian lives a godly life and truly seeks the material and spiritual welfare of those around him, and then is hated and persecuted, his love is put to the test. Our natural tendency is to extend love to those who reciprocate, and to be kind to those who appreciate what we do. It isn't easy to have a genuine and unselfish concern for wicked people with whom we have little in common, even though we know this is what God expects of us. But we find ourselves rebelling against the idea of loving those who hate us and praying for people who abuse us. Yet this is precisely what the Lord Jesus Christ demanded when He said,

> Ye have heard that it hath been said, Thou shalt love thy neighbor, and hate thine enemy;
> But I say unto you, Love your enemies, bless them that curse you, do good to them that hate you, and pray for them who despitefully use you, and persecute you,
> That ye may be the sons of your Father, who is in heaven; for he maketh his sun to rise on the evil and on the good, and sendeth rain on the just and on the unjust (Matthew 5:43-45).

Jesus addresses this command to those who believe on Him, for a person who has not received the Holy Spirit cannot possess this unconquerable benevolence. This grace is possessed only by those who through faith have received a new life, having been united with the Lord Jesus. Since God has graciously saved us, we are responsible to show this invincible goodwill toward others, no matter what they say about us or what they do to us.

If you pray sincerely for your enemies, it will be impossible for you to hate them. You will view them as fellow members of the sinful human family; you will realize that you yourself possess the same natural tendencies; and you will acknowledge that apart from God's grace you too would be an enemy of the truth. You will also believe that Christ died for those who hate you, and have confidence in God's willingness and ability to forgive them and change their lives. Therefore, you will not become bitter, nor will you cease to pray in their behalf.

Yes, even when those who hate Christ are in a position of power, and when they use this authority to imprison or execute His followers, the child of God is to emulate the Lord when He prayed for those who crucified Him, "Father, forgive them; for they know not what they do" (Luke 23:34). This is what Stephen did when a group of men, their eyes flashing fire and their faces reflecting their deep hatred, rushed him outside the city and began to stone him. This young believer, on his knees as the rocks began to pummel his body, lifted his eyes to Heaven in one final appeal, not praying for deliverance but for mercy upon his executioners, "Lord, lay not this sin to their charge" (Acts 7:60).

Christian friend, this is God's way for you to live with those who hate you. You must love them and pray for them no matter what they do. And you may be certain that if you follow our Lord's admonition and example, His cause will prosper. Thousands will be impressed by what they see in us, be convicted of their sin by the Holy Spirit, and believe on Christ. The history of the apostolic church proves that when Christians love their enemies, the power of the Gospel is displayed. A handful of believers were able to turn the world of their day upside down in a period of a few short years. The same grace and strength they manifested is available to us. Let us therefore determine that by God's grace we will indeed love our enemies, pray for them, and seek their good.